AMPLIFIED VOICES

SPEECHES OF WOMEN THAT ASTONISHED THE WORLD

DR. MINAKSHI BANSAL

DEDICATION

To the women who have bravely spoken out, to those who continue to fight for justice, and to the future generations of women who will carry the torch forward.

This book is dedicated to your strength, your resilience, and your unwavering commitment to making the world a better place.

ﭪﭪﭪ

Contents

Prayer   *vii*

About The Author   *ix*

Preface   *xiii*

1. The Power Of Words   1

Part 1

2. Susan B. Anthony: The Fight For Women's Suffrage   9

Part 2

3. Eleanor Roosevelt: The Universal Declaration Of Human   17
Rights

Part 3

4. Indira Gandhi: A Voice For India's Progress   25

Part 4

5. Malala Yousafzai: A Cry For Education   33

Part 5

6. Margaret Thatcher: The Iron Lady's Resolve   41

Part 6

7. Angela Merkel: Leadership In Crisis   49

Part 7

8. Aung San Suu Kyi: The Quest For Democracy   55

Part 8

9. Michelle Obama: Empowering The Next Generation   65

Part 9

10. Greta Thunberg: The Voice Of Climate Change   73

Part 10

11. Jacinda Ardern: Compassionate Leadership   81

Part 11

Contents

12. Benazir Bhutto: A Vision For Pakistan 89

Part 12

13. Wangari Maathai: The Green Belt Movement 97

Part 13

14. Emma Watson: HeForShe Campaign 105

Part 14

15. Ruth Bader Ginsburg: Justice And Equality 113

Part 15

16. Leymah Gbowee: Peace And Reconciliation 121

Part 16

17. Hillary Clinton: Women's Rights Are Human Rights 129

Part 17

18. Ellen Johnson Sirleaf: Leading Liberia 137

Part 18

19. Shirin Ebadi: Advocating For Human Rights In Iran 145

Part 19

20. The Future Of Women's Voices 153

Part 20

21. SUMMARY 161

Citation and References 167

Other Books of the Author 169

CONTACT 175

Prayer

"Om Bhadram Karnebhih Shrinuyama Devah

Bhadram Pashyemakshabhiryajatrah

Sthirairangais Tushtuvamsastanubhih

Vyashema Devahitam Yadayuh

Svasti Na Indro Vriddhashravah

Svasti Nah Pusha Vishwavedah

Svasti Nastarkshyo Arishtanemih

Svasti No Brihaspatir Dadhatu

Om Shantih Shantih Shantih"

This mantra is a prayer for universal well-being, invoking the blessings of various deities for protection, health, and happiness. It emphasizes the importance of experiencing the auspicious through all senses and living a life aligned with divine purpose. The repetition of "Shantih" at the end signifies a deep desire for peace in the individual, the environment, and the universe at large. This mantra is often recited as a prayer for peace, prosperity, and the physical and spiritual well-being of all beings.

ᖇᖇᖇ

About The Author

This book represents the culmination of extensive research and meticulous analysis, incorporating a diverse range of sources, including numerous books, scholarly studies, and personal experiences. Additionally, I have scoured various websites to gather relevant information and data essential for the compilation of this work. I have taken every precaution to ensure the accuracy of the information presented and have diligently cited all sources to acknowledge their contributions.

From her earliest days, Minakshi was distinguished by an insatiable appetite for reading. Her literary universe was inhabited by characters and narratives that spanned ethical tales, motivational and inspirational stories, and the mythic parables imbued with life lessons. This voracious reading habit was not merely for personal edification but was driven by a desire to distill and disseminate the essence of these narratives to foster the development of students and peers alike. She was particularly captivated by the lives and teachings of historical figures and spiritual leaders such as Adi Shankaracharya, Swami Vivekananda, Dr. APJ Abdul Kalam, Mahamana Pandit Madan Mohan Malviya, Mahatma Gandhi, Sardar Vallabhai Patel, and Vinoba Bhave, among others. Their philosophies and life stories fueled her ambition to embody their ideals of resilience, selflessness, and relentless pursuit of knowledge.

Dr. Minakshi's academic and practical engagement with psychology has been equally noteworthy. As a research scholar, her focus has been on exploring the intricate tapestry of the human psyche, aiming to unlock the potential for psychological well-being and societal harmony. Her scholarly work is complemented by her active involvement in social work, where she employs her academic insights to make tangible differences in the lives of the underprivileged. Her endeavours in social work are characterized by an innovative approach that combines traditional wisdom with contemporary psychological practices to address the multifaceted challenges faced by these communities.

Her artistic talents, another facet of her diverse capabilities, are not merely a personal passion but also serve as a medium through which she communicates and connects with others. Her art, rich in symbolism and emotional depth, reflects her philosophical inquiries and social concerns, offering viewers a glimpse into the breadth of her intellect and the depth of her compassion.

In addition to her contributions to the arts and social sciences, Dr. Minakshi has embraced the healing arts of Pranic Healing, mastering the techniques developed by Master Choa Kok Sui. This practice, which focuses on the manipulation of Prana or life energy to heal the body and aura, has been both a personal journey of discovery and a means through which she extends her healing touch to others. Her proficiency in Pranic Healing is complemented by her advocacy and teaching of various forms of meditation aimed at rejuvenation, personal betterment, and the cultivation of harmony within individuals and communities alike.

Dr. Minakshi's life is a narrative of relentless pursuit, not just of personal achievement but of the upliftment and empowerment of society at large. Her diverse interests and talents—spanning the arts, literature, psychology, and the healing practices—converge on a singular path of service. She embodies the spirit of the luminaries who inspired her, channelling their legacy through her actions and teachings. Through her books, art, and social initiatives, she continues to inspire a new generation to embark on their own journeys of self-discovery, resilience, and altruism.

Her commitment to social betterment, particularly her focus on uplifting underprivileged children, reflects a deep understanding of the transformative potential of education and personal development. By integrating her knowledge of psychology, her artistic sensibilities, and her healing practices, Dr. Bansal has developed a holistic approach to social work that addresses both the immediate needs and the long-term well-being of the communities she serves.

As an author, Dr. Minakshi's writings offer a blend of inspirational insights, practical wisdom, and reflective contemplations drawn from her extensive reading and life experiences. Her books serve as a guide for those seeking to navigate the complexities of life with grace, resilience, and purpose. Through her narratives, she extends an invitation to her readers to explore the depths of their own potential and to contribute meaningfully to the collective well-being of society.

In Dr. Minakshi Bansal, we find a remarkable synthesis of the artist, the scholar, the healer, and the social activist. Her life's work stands as a beacon of hope and a source of inspiration for individuals seeking to make a difference in the world. Her story is a compelling reminder of the power of individual action, rooted in compassion and driven by a profound commitment to the betterment of humanity. Dr. Minakshi's legacy is not just in the tangible outcomes of her efforts but in the enduring spirit of inquiry, empathy, and service that she embodies.

ϸϸϸ

Preface

The journey to create this collection has been a deeply personal and profoundly inspiring experience. In a world where women's voices have often been marginalized or silenced, the speeches included in this book represent a powerful testament to the resilience, courage, and unwavering determination of women who have stood up, spoken out, and made a significant impact on history. As I embarked on this project, I was driven by a desire to honor these women and to ensure that their voices continue to resonate, inspiring future generations to continue the fight for equality, justice, and human rights.

Growing up, I was surrounded by stories of remarkable women who defied societal norms and expectations to pursue their dreams and advocate for change. These stories were not just tales of individual achievement; they were narratives of collective struggle, resilience, and triumph. They taught me that the power of a single voice can ignite movements, challenge oppressive systems, and inspire others to action. This understanding shaped my worldview and fueled my passion for highlighting the contributions of women who have made a difference through their words and actions.

In my research for this book, I was struck by the diversity of experiences and perspectives represented by the women whose speeches are featured here. From political leaders and human rights activists to environmentalists and gender equality advocates, these women come from different backgrounds, cultures, and contexts. Yet, despite their differences, they share a common thread: a profound commitment to justice, equality, and the betterment of humanity. Their speeches are a reflection of their unique journeys and the values they hold dear. They challenge us to reflect on our own beliefs, question the status quo, and envision a world where everyone's voice is heard and valued.

One of the most compelling aspects of these speeches is their ability to transcend time and place. While each speech is rooted in a specific context, the themes they address—freedom, equality, justice, and human dignity—are universal. The words of these women resonate across borders and generations, reminding us of the ongoing struggle for a more just and equitable world. As I delved into their stories, I was reminded of the power of language to inspire change, to mobilize communities, and to transform societies. These speeches are not just historical artifacts; they are living documents that continue to inspire and motivate.

In compiling this book, I was particularly moved by the personal sacrifices many of these women have made in their pursuit of justice and equality. Their journeys are often marked by significant personal risk, loss, and hardship. Yet, despite these challenges, they have remained steadfast in their commitment to their causes. Their resilience is a testament to the strength of the human spirit and the enduring power of hope. Their stories remind us that progress is often achieved through perseverance and that meaningful change requires courage and determination.

As I reflect on the process of creating this book, I am reminded of the importance of representation and visibility. For too long, the contributions of women have been overlooked or minimized in historical narratives. By amplifying the voices of these remarkable women, I hope to contribute to a more inclusive and accurate representation of history. Their speeches serve as powerful reminders of the critical role women have played—and continue to play—in shaping our world. They challenge us to recognize and celebrate the contributions of women in all spheres of life and to work towards a future where gender equality is not just an aspiration but a reality.

The women featured in this book have used their voices to advocate for a wide range of issues, from gender equality and human rights to environmental sustainability and social justice. Their speeches address some of the most pressing challenges of our time, offering insights, solutions, and calls to action. They remind us that the fight for justice is multifaceted and that progress in one area often intersects with progress in others. By highlighting their diverse contributions, I hope to underscore the interconnectedness of these struggles and the importance of a holistic approach to social change.

In writing this book, I have been inspired by the legacy of the women whose speeches are included here. Their words have challenged me to think more deeply about my own values and actions and to consider how I can contribute to the ongoing fight for justice and equality. Their courage and determination have been a source of motivation, reminding me that each of us has the power to make a difference. Their speeches are a call to action, urging us to use our voices, our talents, and our resources to advocate for a more just and equitable world.

As we look to the future, it is essential that we continue to amplify the voices of women and to create spaces where their contributions are recognized and valued. This book is a step towards that goal, but it is by no means the end of the journey. There are countless women whose voices have yet to be heard, whose stories have yet to be told. By continuing to listen, to learn, and to advocate, we can ensure that the legacy of these remarkable women lives on and that their vision for a better world becomes a reality.

The process of creating this book has been a labor of love, driven by a deep respect for the women whose voices it seeks to amplify. It has been a journey of discovery, reflection, and inspiration. I am profoundly grateful to the women whose speeches are featured here for their courage, their wisdom, and their unwavering commitment to justice. Their words have touched my heart, challenged my mind, and inspired my soul. It is my hope that this book will do the same for its readers, offering a source of inspiration, motivation, and empowerment.

In conclusion, the voices of the women featured in this book are a powerful reminder of the transformative potential of language and the enduring impact of advocacy. Their speeches are a testament to the strength, resilience, and determination of women who have dedicated their lives to the pursuit of justice and equality. As we listen to their words, may we be inspired to continue their work, to amplify their voices, and to strive for a world where everyone's voice is heard and valued. This book is a celebration of their contributions, a tribute to their legacy, and a call to action for all of us to use our voices for positive change.

Dr. Minakshi Bansal
Social Activist
Ahmedabad, Gujarat, Bharat

ϷϷϷ

ONE
The Power of Words

Words have an undeniable power to shape our world, influence minds, and alter the course of history. Throughout time, the spoken word has served as a catalyst for change, a tool for empowerment, and a means of expressing profound ideas. The power of words is especially evident in the speeches of remarkable women who have used their voices to inspire, challenge, and lead. These speeches are not just moments in history; they are echoes of passion, resilience, and a deep commitment to making the world a better place.

The significance of words lies in their ability to convey complex emotions, ideas, and visions. When spoken with conviction and sincerity, words can move hearts and minds. This is particularly true for speeches, where the speaker's tone, pace, and presence add layers of meaning to the words themselves. A powerful speech can galvanize a movement, bring attention to injustices, and offer hope in times of despair. The ability to articulate thoughts clearly and persuasively is a skill that has been honed by many influential women throughout history.

One of the most compelling aspects of powerful speeches is their ability to transcend time and place. The words of women like Susan

B. Anthony, Malala Yousafzai, and Eleanor Roosevelt resonate across generations, continuing to inspire and motivate. These women understood the importance of their words and used them to advocate for causes they believed in deeply. Their speeches were not just expressions of personal beliefs but calls to action for others to join them in their fight for justice, equality, and human rights.

Susan B. Anthony, for instance, used her speeches to advocate for women's suffrage in the United States. Her eloquence and determination helped to galvanize the movement for women's rights, and her words continue to inspire activists today. Anthony's speeches were characterized by their clarity, passion, and unwavering commitment to the cause of women's equality. She understood that the right to vote was not just a political issue but a fundamental human right, and she used her words to make that case to the world.

Similarly, Malala Yousafzai's speeches on the importance of education for girls have had a profound impact on global awareness and action. After surviving an assassination attempt by the Taliban, Malala used her voice to advocate for the millions of girls who are denied the right to education. Her speeches are marked by a powerful blend of personal experience, moral conviction, and a vision for a better future. Malala's words have not only brought attention to the plight of girls around the world but have also inspired countless individuals to take action in support of education and gender equality.

Eleanor Roosevelt, another iconic figure, used her speeches to champion human rights and social justice. As a leading figure in the drafting of the Universal Declaration of Human Rights, Roosevelt's words helped to shape the framework for international human rights law. Her speeches were characterized by their depth of understanding, compassion, and a profound sense of duty to humanity. Roosevelt's ability to articulate the principles of human rights in a way that resonated with people from all walks of life was a testament to the power of her words.

The impact of powerful speeches is not limited to political and social movements. In times of crisis, leaders' words can provide comfort, reassurance, and a sense of direction. During the COVID-19 pandemic, leaders like Angela Merkel delivered speeches that were praised for their clarity, honesty, and empathy. Merkel's speeches during the crisis emphasized the importance of solidarity, science, and collective responsibility. Her calm and measured words provided a sense of stability and trust during uncertain times, illustrating how effective communication can play a crucial role in managing crises.

The speeches of these remarkable women also highlight the intersection of personal experience and public advocacy. Many of these women drew upon their own life experiences to inform their speeches and connect with their audiences. This personal connection adds authenticity and emotional weight to their words, making their messages even more compelling. For example, Malala Yousafzai's personal story of surviving an attack for her advocacy adds a powerful dimension to her speeches on education. Similarly, Eleanor Roosevelt's own experiences with loss, hardship, and public service informed her passionate advocacy for human rights.

The power of words is also evident in the way they can challenge existing norms and inspire new ways of thinking. Margaret Thatcher, known as the "Iron Lady," used her speeches to challenge the status quo and promote her vision of conservative policies. Her speeches were often controversial, but they were also instrumental in shaping public debate and policy. Thatcher's ability to articulate her ideas forcefully and persuasively helped to redefine the political landscape in Britain and beyond.

In contrast, speeches by figures like Greta Thunberg have

challenged the world to rethink its approach to climate change. Thunberg's speeches are characterized by their blunt honesty, emotional intensity, and urgent call to action. Her words have galvanized a global movement of young people demanding action on climate change, illustrating how the power of words can drive social and environmental change. Thunberg's speeches highlight the importance of speaking truth to power and the impact that a single voice can have in raising awareness and inspiring collective action.

The power of words extends beyond the content of the speeches themselves to the way they are delivered. The effectiveness of a speech is often enhanced by the speaker's ability to connect with their audience, convey their passion, and use rhetorical techniques to emphasize their points. Techniques such as repetition, storytelling, and rhetorical questions can make speeches more memorable and impactful. For example, Martin Luther King Jr.'s use of repetition in his famous "I Have a Dream" speech helped to reinforce his message and make it more resonant with his audience.

In addition to rhetorical techniques, the context in which a speech is delivered can also influence its impact. Speeches delivered at critical moments in history, such as during times of social upheaval, war, or crisis, can have a particularly profound effect. The timing and setting of a speech can amplify its significance and reach. For example, Winston Churchill's speeches during World War II were delivered at a time when Britain was facing existential threats, and his words helped to rally the nation and boost morale. Similarly, speeches delivered at key moments in social movements, such as the civil rights movement, have played a crucial role in mobilizing support and driving change.

The speeches of women who have astonished the world often reflect a deep understanding of the power of words and their potential to effect change. These women have used their voices to advocate for justice, equality, and human rights, and their speeches continue to inspire and motivate people around the world. Their words serve as a reminder of the importance of using one's voice to speak out against injustice and to strive for a better world.

In the context of education, the power of words is also evident in the way teachers and educators use language to inspire and motivate students. The words of a passionate teacher can ignite a love of learning, encourage critical thinking, and foster a sense of curiosity and wonder. Educators who use their words effectively can create a positive and supportive learning environment, helping students to develop confidence and a sense of purpose. The influence of teachers' words on their students' lives is a testament to the broader impact that powerful speech can have in shaping minds and futures.

The power of words is not limited to formal speeches but can also be seen in everyday interactions and conversations. The words we choose in our daily lives can have a significant impact on our relationships, our sense of self, and our ability to influence others. Kind words can uplift and encourage, while hurtful words can cause lasting damage. The ability to communicate effectively and empathetically is a valuable skill that can enhance personal and professional relationships.

In the digital age, the power of words has taken on new dimensions with the rise of social media and online communication. Platforms like Twitter, Facebook, and Instagram allow individuals to reach a global audience with their words, amplifying their impact. The digital landscape has created new opportunities for advocacy and activism, as well as new challenges in managing the spread of misinformation and harmful speech. The power of words in the digital age underscores the importance of using language responsibly and ethically.

The enduring impact of powerful speeches by women who have astonished the world highlights the importance of continuing to amplify diverse voices and perspectives. As society evolves, new challenges and opportunities will arise, and the need for strong, articulate voices advocating for justice, equality, and human rights will remain. By studying and celebrating the speeches of remarkable women, we can draw inspiration from their courage, wisdom, and vision, and apply those lessons to the challenges we face today.

In conclusion, the power of words is a fundamental aspect of human communication and a key driver of social change. The speeches of remarkable women throughout history demonstrate the profound impact that well-chosen words can have in shaping our world. These women have used their voices to advocate for important causes, challenge the status quo, and inspire others to join them in their pursuit of a more just and equitable society. Their speeches serve as a testament to the enduring power of words and the importance of using our voices to make a positive difference in the world.

"In the symphony of life, every note carries the melody of our journey, weaving tales of triumph and tribulation, painting the canvas of our existence with hues of resilience."

TWO

SUSAN B. ANTHONY: THE FIGHT FOR WOMEN'S SUFFRAGE

Susan B. Anthony is a name synonymous with the fight for women's suffrage in the United States. Her tireless efforts, powerful speeches, and unwavering dedication to the cause of women's rights left an indelible mark on American history. Anthony's work transcended the boundaries of her time, laying the groundwork for the eventual success of the women's suffrage movement and inspiring future generations of activists. Her speeches, in particular, were a critical component of her advocacy, providing a platform to articulate her vision, challenge societal norms, and mobilize support for women's right to vote.

Born on February 15, 1820, in Adams, Massachusetts, Susan B. Anthony grew up in a Quaker family that valued education and social justice. Her upbringing instilled in her a sense of duty to fight for equality and human rights. Early on, she became involved in the temperance movement, which sought to curb the consumption of alcohol, but soon realized that her efforts were hampered by the lack of political power granted to women. This realization propelled her into the women's rights movement, where she would become one of its most prominent leaders.

Anthony's partnership with Elizabeth Cady Stanton was instrumental in advancing the cause of women's suffrage. Together, they formed a formidable team, with Stanton often focusing on writing and strategy while Anthony took on the role of public speaker and organizer. Anthony's ability to engage with diverse audiences and articulate the injustices faced by women made her an effective advocate for the movement. Her speeches were marked by their clarity, logical structure, and emotional appeal, which resonated deeply with her listeners.

One of Anthony's most famous speeches, delivered in 1873, came after her arrest for voting illegally in the 1872 presidential election. Defiant and resolute, Anthony argued that her right to vote was guaranteed by the Constitution. She invoked the preamble, stating, "We, the people of the United States," emphasizing that women were part of "the people" and therefore entitled to the same rights as men. This speech, delivered with conviction and passion, highlighted the hypocrisy of a democratic nation that excluded half its population from participating in the political process. Anthony's words not only challenged the legal system but also galvanized public opinion in favor of women's suffrage.

Anthony's speeches often employed a mix of moral and logical arguments to make her case. She drew parallels between the fight for women's suffrage and other struggles for justice, such as the abolition of slavery. By aligning the women's rights movement with broader principles of equality and human rights, she sought to demonstrate that denying women the right to vote was not only unjust but also fundamentally un-American. Her speeches were designed to appeal to both the hearts and minds of her audience, urging them to consider the moral implications of their stance on women's suffrage.

Throughout her life, Anthony faced significant opposition and hostility. She was often ridiculed and attacked for her views, yet she remained undeterred. Her resilience in the face of adversity was a testament to her deep commitment to the cause. Anthony's speeches were not just expressions of her beliefs but acts of courage that defied societal norms and challenged the status quo. Her willingness to stand up and speak out, even when it was dangerous or unpopular, inspired others to join the movement and continue the fight for women's rights.

Anthony's advocacy extended beyond speeches and public appearances. She was a prolific writer, using her pen to further the cause of women's suffrage. She co-founded and edited "The Revolution," a weekly newspaper dedicated to women's rights, which provided a platform for discussing issues related to gender equality, social justice, and political reform. Through her writing, Anthony reached a wider audience, disseminating her ideas and mobilizing support for the movement. Her ability to communicate effectively, both in speech and in writing, was a key factor in the success of the women's suffrage movement.

One of Anthony's notable achievements was her role in organizing and leading the National Woman Suffrage Association (NWSA), which she co-founded with Stanton in 1869. The NWSA played a critical role in advocating for a constitutional amendment to grant women the right to vote. Anthony traveled extensively, giving speeches, organizing rallies, and lobbying lawmakers to support women's suffrage. Her tireless efforts helped to build a broad coalition of supporters and bring the issue of women's voting rights to the forefront of national politics.

Anthony's strategic approach to advocacy also included forging alliances with other social reform movements. She understood that the fight for women's suffrage was interconnected with other struggles for justice and sought to build bridges with movements for labor rights, civil rights, and education reform. By aligning the women's suffrage movement with these broader social causes, Anthony sought to create a united front for change. Her ability to connect with diverse groups and build coalitions was a testament to her leadership and vision.

Despite her many accomplishments, Anthony did not live to see the culmination of her efforts. She passed away in 1906, fourteen years before the ratification of the 19th Amendment in 1920, which granted women the right to vote. However, her legacy lived on through the countless activists and supporters she had inspired. The passage of the 19th Amendment was a direct result of the groundwork laid by Anthony and her contemporaries, who had dedicated their lives to the cause of women's suffrage.

Anthony's impact on the women's suffrage movement cannot be overstated. Her speeches, writings, and organizational efforts were pivotal in advancing the cause and achieving the eventual success of the movement. Her ability to articulate the principles of justice and equality, challenge societal norms, and mobilize support was instrumental in changing public opinion and securing political rights for women. Anthony's legacy is a testament to the power of words and the importance of using one's voice to advocate for justice and equality.

The fight for women's suffrage was a long and arduous journey, marked by moments of triumph and setbacks. Anthony's speeches were a source of inspiration and motivation for those who continued the struggle after her death. Her words served as a reminder of the importance of perseverance and the need to remain steadfast in the pursuit of justice. The principles she articulated and the vision she championed continue to resonate with activists and advocates for women's rights today.

In reflecting on Anthony's contributions, it is important to recognize the broader impact of her work on the women's rights movement. Her efforts helped to lay the foundation for subsequent waves of feminism and the ongoing struggle for gender equality. Anthony's advocacy for women's suffrage was not just about securing the right to vote but also about challenging the broader system of gender inequality and advocating for women's full participation in society. Her vision extended beyond the ballot box, encompassing issues such as education, employment, and social justice.

Anthony's life and work also highlight the importance of leadership and collaboration in social movements. Her partnership with Elizabeth Cady Stanton and her ability to build alliances with other reform movements were crucial to the success of the women's suffrage movement. Anthony's leadership was characterized by a combination of strategic vision, effective communication, and unwavering dedication to the cause. Her ability to inspire and mobilize others was a key factor in the movement's achievements.

As we look back on Anthony's legacy, it is important to consider the lessons her life and work offer for contemporary activism. The fight for women's suffrage was a struggle that required perseverance, resilience, and a willingness to challenge deeply entrenched social norms. Anthony's ability to use her voice to advocate for justice and mobilize support serves as a powerful example for today's activists. Her legacy reminds us of the importance of speaking out against injustice, building broad coalitions for change, and remaining committed to the pursuit of equality and human rights.

The enduring impact of Anthony's speeches is a testament to the power of words to effect change. Her ability to articulate a vision of equality and justice, challenge societal norms, and inspire others to join the movement was instrumental in advancing the cause of women's suffrage. Anthony's speeches continue to resonate with us today, serving as a reminder of the importance of using our voices to advocate for justice and equality.

In conclusion, Susan B. Anthony's contributions to the fight for women's suffrage were marked by her powerful speeches, strategic vision, and unwavering dedication to the cause of women's rights. Her ability to articulate the principles of justice and equality, challenge societal norms, and mobilize support was instrumental in changing public opinion and securing political rights for women. Anthony's legacy is a testament to the power of words and the importance of using one's voice to advocate for justice and equality. Her life and work continue to inspire and guide us in the ongoing struggle for gender equality and human rights.

ᐳᐳᐳ

"Like stars in the vast expanse of the night sky, our dreams twinkle with the promise of possibility, guiding us through the darkness with their luminous grace."

THREE

ELEANOR ROOSEVELT: THE UNIVERSAL DECLARATION OF HUMAN RIGHTS

Eleanor Roosevelt, a towering figure in the annals of human rights, played a pivotal role in the creation of the Universal Declaration of Human Rights (UDHR). Her journey toward this monumental achievement was marked by a deep commitment to social justice, an unwavering belief in the inherent dignity of every individual, and a tireless effort to promote peace and equality on a global scale. Her contributions to the UDHR were not just political but deeply personal, reflecting her lifelong dedication to the principles of human rights and her ability to inspire and mobilize people around these ideals.

Born on October 11, 1884, Eleanor Roosevelt's early life was shaped by both privilege and tragedy. She was born into a prominent family, but her childhood was marred by the loss of both parents by the time she was ten years old. These early experiences of loss and hardship imbued her with a deep sense of empathy and a desire to help those in need. Eleanor married Franklin D. Roosevelt in 1905, and their partnership would become one of the most influential in American history. As First Lady of the United States from 1933 to 1945, Eleanor redefined the role, using her position to champion social causes and advocate for the marginalized.

Eleanor's involvement in the United Nations and the drafting of the UDHR began after World War II, a period marked by widespread devastation and a global commitment to preventing such atrocities in the future. In 1946, she was appointed as a delegate to the United Nations General Assembly by President Harry S. Truman. Soon after, she became the chair of the UN Commission on Human Rights, a position that would place her at the forefront of the effort to articulate a global standard for human rights.

The drafting of the UDHR was a complex and collaborative process involving representatives from various countries and cultures, each bringing their own perspectives and priorities to the table. Eleanor's role as chair was crucial in navigating these diverse viewpoints and building consensus. Her diplomatic skills, patience, and ability to listen were instrumental in fostering an environment where constructive dialogue could occur. She understood the importance of creating a document that was both universally applicable and reflective of the shared values of humanity.

One of Eleanor's significant contributions to the UDHR was her emphasis on the universality of human rights. She believed that human rights were not confined by national borders or cultural differences but were inherent to all people, regardless of their background. This conviction was reflected in her efforts to ensure that the Declaration encompassed a broad range of rights, including civil, political, economic, social, and cultural rights. She recognized that true human dignity required not only freedom from oppression and violence but also access to basic necessities such as food, education, and healthcare.

Eleanor's speeches and writings during this period provide valuable insights into her vision for the UDHR. She often spoke about the interconnectedness of human rights, arguing that civil and political rights were meaningless without economic and social rights, and vice versa. Her ability to articulate these ideas in a clear and compelling manner helped to garner widespread support for the Declaration. She was adept at using her platform to educate the public about the importance of human rights and to inspire a sense of collective responsibility for their protection.

One of the key challenges in drafting the UDHR was balancing the aspirations of the Declaration with the political realities of the time. The early years of the Cold War were marked by ideological tensions between the Western bloc, led by the United States, and the Eastern bloc, led by the Soviet Union. These tensions often played out in debates over the content of the Declaration, with different countries advocating for provisions that aligned with their political philosophies. Eleanor's leadership was crucial in navigating these ideological divides and finding common ground. She was committed to creating a document that would be acceptable to as many countries as possible while remaining true to the core principles of human rights.

Eleanor's ability to build consensus was evident in the final adoption of the UDHR by the UN General Assembly on December 10, 1948. The Declaration was adopted by a vote of 48 in favor, with none against and eight abstentions. This near-unanimous support was a testament to Eleanor's diplomatic skills and her ability to bring people together around a shared vision. The UDHR represented a milestone in the history of human rights, providing a comprehensive framework for the protection and promotion of human dignity.

The text of the UDHR itself is a reflection of Eleanor's inclusive and holistic approach to human rights. The preamble sets the tone by affirming the "inherent dignity" and "equal and inalienable rights of all members of the human family." The 30 articles that follow outline a wide range of rights, including the right to life, liberty, and security; freedom from torture and arbitrary detention; freedom of thought, conscience, and religion; and the right to work, education, and an adequate standard of living. The Declaration's comprehensive scope underscores the interconnectedness of different types of rights and the importance of addressing all aspects of human well-being.

Eleanor's legacy in the field of human rights extends beyond the adoption of the UDHR. She continued to be an active advocate for human rights until her death in 1962, using her platform to speak out on issues such as racial equality, women's rights, and social justice. Her work with the United Nations and other organizations helped to lay the groundwork for subsequent human rights instruments and institutions, including the International Covenant on Civil and Political Rights and the International Covenant on Economic, Social and Cultural Rights.

Eleanor's impact on the human rights movement is also reflected in the way she inspired future generations of activists and leaders. Her dedication to the cause, her ability to articulate a vision for a more just and equitable world, and her commitment to building bridges across cultural and political divides serve as enduring examples for those who continue to fight for human rights today. Eleanor's work reminds us of the importance of perseverance, empathy, and collaboration in the pursuit of justice.

The UDHR remains a foundational document in the field of human rights, serving as a benchmark against which the actions of governments and other actors can be measured. Its principles have been incorporated into numerous national constitutions and international treaties, and it continues to be a powerful tool for advocacy and education. The Declaration's enduring relevance is a testament to the vision and dedication of Eleanor Roosevelt and her colleagues.

Eleanor's contributions to the UDHR were not limited to her formal role as chair of the Commission on Human Rights. Her personal experiences and values deeply influenced her work. She often drew upon her own encounters with discrimination and injustice to inform her advocacy. For example, her experiences with segregation and racial discrimination in the United States fueled her commitment to promoting racial equality on a global scale. Her travels around the world, where she witnessed firsthand the impact of poverty and oppression, reinforced her belief in the importance of economic and social rights.

Eleanor's ability to connect with people from different backgrounds and to understand their struggles was one of her greatest strengths as a human rights advocate. She was known for her humility, approachability, and genuine concern for others. These qualities enabled her to build strong relationships with her colleagues and to foster a sense of trust and collaboration. Her leadership style was characterized by inclusivity and respect for diverse perspectives, which was crucial in the context of the international negotiations over the UDHR.

One of the enduring lessons from Eleanor's work on the UDHR is the importance of principled leadership. She demonstrated that effective leadership in the field of human rights requires not only intellectual and diplomatic skills but also a deep commitment to ethical principles. Her ability to stay true to her values, even in the face of political pressures and challenges, was a key factor in her success. Eleanor's leadership was guided by a profound belief in the dignity and worth of every individual, and this belief was reflected in every aspect of her work.

Eleanor Roosevelt's legacy in the field of human rights is a powerful reminder of the impact that one individual can have in advancing the cause of justice and equality. Her contributions to the UDHR were a culmination of a lifetime of advocacy and activism, and they continue to inspire and guide us today. As we reflect on her achievements, we are reminded of the importance of continuing the fight for human rights and of the enduring power of the principles she championed.

In summary, Eleanor Roosevelt's role in the creation of the Universal Declaration of Human Rights was a testament to her dedication, vision, and leadership. Her ability to build consensus, articulate a comprehensive vision for human rights, and inspire others to join the cause were instrumental in the adoption of the UDHR. Eleanor's legacy continues to resonate today, reminding us of the importance of perseverance, empathy, and principled leadership in the pursuit of justice. The UDHR remains a foundational document in the field of human rights, and its enduring relevance is a tribute to Eleanor Roosevelt's tireless efforts and unwavering commitment to the principles of human dignity and equality.

$$\wp\wp\wp$$

"Amidst the chaos of uncertainty, find solace in the whispers of your own strength, for within you lies the power to carve pathways from the rock of adversity."

FOUR

INDIRA GANDHI: A VOICE FOR INDIA'S PROGRESS

Indira Gandhi, one of India's most influential and controversial leaders, played a pivotal role in shaping the country's progress during the mid-20th century. As the first and, to date, only female Prime Minister of India, her tenure was marked by significant achievements and profound challenges. Her voice for India's progress was characterized by her determination, resilience, and an unyielding vision for a self-reliant and modern nation. Indira Gandhi's leadership was a blend of political acumen, strategic foresight, and an understanding of India's socio-economic complexities.

Born on November 19, 1917, in Allahabad, India, Indira Gandhi was the daughter of Jawaharlal Nehru, the first Prime Minister of independent India, and Kamala Nehru, an active participant in India's freedom struggle. Growing up in a politically charged environment, Indira was exposed to the ideals of nationalism and the quest for independence from an early age. Her education at institutions such as Visva-Bharati University in India and the

University of Oxford in the United Kingdom provided her with a broad perspective on global politics and the challenges facing newly independent nations.

Indira Gandhi's political career began in earnest when she was elected as the President of the Indian National Congress in 1959. Her rise within the party was not just a result of her lineage but also her deep understanding of India's political landscape and her ability to connect with the masses. In 1966, following the untimely death of Prime Minister Lal Bahadur Shastri, Indira Gandhi was elected as the Prime Minister of India, marking the beginning of a transformative era in Indian politics.

One of Indira Gandhi's most notable contributions to India's progress was her focus on self-reliance and modernization. She championed the Green Revolution, a series of initiatives aimed at increasing agricultural productivity through the use of high-yielding variety seeds, modern irrigation techniques, and chemical fertilizers. The Green Revolution transformed India from a food-deficient nation to one that was self-sufficient in food production, significantly reducing famine and poverty in rural areas. This initiative not only boosted India's agricultural output but also laid the foundation for economic growth and stability.

Indira Gandhi's tenure was also marked by significant industrial development. She implemented policies aimed at promoting heavy industries and public sector enterprises, believing that a strong industrial base was essential for national progress. Her government nationalized major banks in 1969, a move that aimed to increase credit availability to farmers and small industries, thereby fostering inclusive economic growth. This policy of nationalization was controversial but played a crucial role in ensuring that financial resources were directed towards sectors that needed them the most.

Another key aspect of Indira Gandhi's leadership was her

commitment to social justice and equality. She launched various programs aimed at poverty alleviation, education, and healthcare. Her slogan "Garibi Hatao" (Eradicate Poverty) became the cornerstone of her political campaigns and policies. Indira Gandhi understood that true progress could not be achieved without addressing the socio-economic disparities that plagued Indian society. Her efforts to improve the status of women and marginalized communities were evident in her policies and initiatives.

Indira Gandhi's voice for India's progress was also evident in her foreign policy. She believed in maintaining India's sovereignty and independence in global affairs. Her leadership during the Bangladesh Liberation War in 1971 was a testament to her strategic acumen and diplomatic skills. By providing support to the Mukti Bahini and managing international pressures, she played a crucial role in the creation of Bangladesh, thereby altering the geopolitical landscape of South Asia. This decisive action not only bolstered India's position in the region but also demonstrated her ability to take bold steps in the interest of national security and humanitarianism.

Despite her many achievements, Indira Gandhi's tenure was not without controversy. Her declaration of the Emergency in 1975, following a period of political unrest and economic instability, remains one of the most debated aspects of her leadership. During the Emergency, civil liberties were suspended, opposition leaders were imprisoned, and the press was censored. While Indira Gandhi argued that these measures were necessary to restore order and implement urgent reforms, critics viewed it as an authoritarian move that undermined democratic principles. The Emergency period left a complex legacy, with some arguing that it showcased her decisive leadership, while others saw it as a dark chapter in India's democratic history.

Indira Gandhi's leadership style was often described as charismatic and authoritative. She was known for her ability to connect with the masses and her unwavering determination to achieve her vision for India. Her speeches and public addresses were powerful tools through which she communicated her ideas and rallied support for her policies. Indira Gandhi's voice resonated with millions of Indians, instilling a sense of national pride and purpose. Her ability to articulate the aspirations and challenges of a diverse nation made her a revered figure in Indian politics.

The later years of Indira Gandhi's tenure were marked by significant challenges, including economic difficulties, political unrest, and security threats. The rise of separatist movements, particularly in Punjab, posed a serious threat to national unity. Her decision to launch Operation Blue Star in 1984, aimed at flushing out militants from the Golden Temple, was a controversial and consequential move. While it was intended to restore order, the operation resulted in significant casualties and deeply hurt the sentiments of the Sikh community. This decision ultimately led to her assassination on October 31, 1984, by her own bodyguards, sparking widespread violence and unrest.

Indira Gandhi's legacy is multifaceted, reflecting both her substantial contributions to India's progress and the contentious aspects of her leadership. Her efforts in modernizing India's agriculture and industry, her commitment to social justice, and her strategic foreign policy initiatives have had a lasting impact on the nation's development. At the same time, the controversies surrounding the Emergency and her handling of political dissent have sparked ongoing debates about the nature of her leadership and its implications for Indian democracy.

Indira Gandhi's influence extends beyond her time in office. She paved the way for future generations of women leaders in India and around the world, demonstrating that women could lead at the highest levels of government and make significant contributions to national and global affairs. Her resilience in the face of adversity, her ability to navigate complex political landscapes, and her unwavering commitment to her vision for India continue to inspire leaders and activists today.

Reflecting on Indira Gandhi's voice for India's progress, it is essential to consider the broader context of her leadership. She governed during a period of immense change and challenge, navigating the complexities of a newly independent nation striving for economic development and social justice. Her ability to balance the demands of modernization with the need to preserve India's cultural heritage and social fabric was a defining aspect of her tenure. Indira Gandhi's leadership was marked by her capacity to envision a self-reliant and prosperous India while addressing the immediate needs and aspirations of its people.

Indira Gandhi's speeches and public addresses provide a window into her vision for India's progress. She often spoke about the importance of self-reliance, unity, and social justice, emphasizing the need for collective effort and national pride. Her rhetoric was designed to inspire and mobilize, instilling a sense of purpose and direction among the Indian populace. Through her words, she sought to bridge the gap between the government's policies and the people's aspirations, fostering a sense of shared destiny and collective responsibility.

One of the enduring aspects of Indira Gandhi's legacy is her ability to connect with diverse sections of Indian society. She understood the importance of inclusive development and worked towards policies that aimed to uplift the marginalized and disadvantaged. Her focus on poverty alleviation, rural development, and women's empowerment reflected her commitment to ensuring that the benefits of progress reached all segments of society. Indira Gandhi's efforts in promoting education, healthcare, and social welfare have had a lasting impact on India's socio-economic landscape.

Indira Gandhi's leadership also highlighted the challenges and complexities of governing a diverse and populous nation like India. Her ability to navigate the intricate dynamics of Indian politics, manage external pressures, and respond to internal challenges was a testament to her political acumen and strategic foresight. While her tenure was marked by both achievements and controversies, it underscored the need for strong and visionary leadership in addressing the multifaceted issues facing the nation.

Indira Gandhi's assassination in 1984 marked the end of an era in Indian politics. Her death was a significant loss for the nation, and the subsequent violence and unrest reflected the deep-seated emotions and divisions within Indian society. However, her legacy endures through the policies she implemented, the progress she championed, and the vision she articulated for India. Indira Gandhi's contributions to India's development and her role as a voice for progress continue to be remembered and debated, reflecting the enduring impact of her leadership.

In conclusion, Indira Gandhi's voice for India's progress was characterized by her determination, vision, and resilience. Her efforts in promoting self-reliance, industrial development, social justice, and strategic foreign policy were instrumental in shaping India's trajectory during a critical period in its history. Despite the controversies and challenges of her tenure, her contributions to India's progress and her role as a pioneering woman leader have left an indelible mark on the nation's history. Indira Gandhi's legacy continues to inspire and guide future generations, reminding us of the importance of visionary leadership, inclusive development, and unwavering commitment to the ideals of progress and justice.

ppp

"In the garden of adversity, resilience blooms as the most exquisite flower, its petals unfurling with each challenge, casting a fragrance of perseverance into the air."

FIVE

MALALA YOUSAFZAI: A CRY FOR EDUCATION

Malala Yousafzai's story is a powerful testament to the strength of the human spirit and the transformative power of education. Born on July 12, 1997, in Mingora, Pakistan, Malala grew up in a region where the Taliban had a significant presence and where girls' education was often met with violent opposition. Despite these challenges, Malala's unwavering commitment to education and her courageous advocacy have made her an international symbol of the fight for girls' right to learn.

Malala's father, Ziauddin Yousafzai, was an educator and an outspoken advocate for education in Pakistan. He ran a chain of schools in the region and was a significant influence on Malala, instilling in her the values of education, equality, and activism from a young age. Ziauddin's encouragement and support played a crucial role in shaping Malala's early views on the importance of education and her willingness to speak out against the injustices faced by girls in her community.

In 2009, when Malala was just 11 years old, she began writing a blog for the BBC Urdu under a pseudonym, documenting her life under Taliban rule and the difficulties girls faced in pursuing education. Her writing provided a rare and insightful perspective on the impact of the Taliban's policies on girls' education in the Swat Valley. Malala's blog gained international attention, highlighting the urgent need to address the barriers to education faced by girls in Pakistan and other conflict-affected regions.

Malala's advocacy did not come without risks. As her profile grew, so did the threats against her and her family. Despite the danger, Malala continued to speak out publicly in favor of girls' education. Her courage and determination to fight for what she believed in were evident in her speeches and public appearances. She believed that education was a fundamental human right and that empowering girls through education was essential for creating a more just and equitable society.

On October 9, 2012, Malala's life changed forever. While riding a bus home from school, she was targeted by a Taliban gunman who shot her in the head. The attack was intended to silence her and deter other girls from pursuing their education. However, it had the opposite effect. Malala's survival and subsequent recovery became a rallying point for advocates of girls' education around the world. The attempted assassination brought global attention to the issue of girls' education and the extreme measures taken by those who opposed it.

Malala was airlifted to Birmingham, United Kingdom, for medical treatment. The world watched as she fought for her life, and her recovery was seen as nothing short of miraculous. During her time in the hospital and subsequent rehabilitation, Malala's resolve to fight for girls' education only grew stronger. She used her experience to draw even more attention to the plight of girls who were denied an education and to advocate for the millions of girls around the world who faced similar threats and challenges.

In 2013, Malala co-authored the memoir "I Am Malala: The Girl Who Stood Up for Education and Was Shot by the Taliban," which detailed her life, the attack, and her continuing advocacy for education. The book became an international bestseller and further amplified her message. Malala's story resonated with people across the globe, inspiring countless individuals to join the fight for girls' education.

Malala's advocacy extended beyond public speaking and writing. In 2013, she and her father founded the Malala Fund, an organization dedicated to advocating for girls' education and empowering young girls to achieve their potential. The Malala Fund supports local education activists and initiatives in countries such as Pakistan, Nigeria, Syria, and India, working to break down the barriers that prevent girls from going to school. The organization focuses on issues such as poverty, gender discrimination, and conflict, which are significant obstacles to girls' education.

Malala's work with the Malala Fund has had a tangible impact on the lives of many girls around the world. By providing resources, support, and advocacy, the organization has helped to ensure that more girls have access to quality education. Malala's vision for the Malala Fund is rooted in the belief that educated girls can transform their communities and contribute to the development of their countries. She sees education as a powerful tool for social change and economic development, and her work reflects her commitment to making this vision a reality.

In 2014, at the age of 17, Malala Yousafzai became the youngest-ever recipient of the Nobel Peace Prize, which she shared with Kailash Satyarthi, an Indian child rights activist. The Nobel Committee recognized Malala's "struggle against the suppression of children and young people and for the right of all children to education."

Receiving the Nobel Peace Prize was a significant milestone in Malala's journey, highlighting the importance of her work and the global recognition of the issues she champions.

Malala's speeches at international forums, including the United Nations, have been powerful calls to action. In her address to the UN Youth Assembly on her 16th birthday, she declared, "One child, one teacher, one book, one pen can change the world." Her words emphasized the transformative power of education and the responsibility of the global community to ensure that every child has the opportunity to learn. Malala's ability to articulate her message with clarity, passion, and conviction has made her an effective advocate and an inspirational figure.

Malala's advocacy for girls' education also addresses broader issues of gender equality and human rights. She has consistently highlighted the link between education and the empowerment of women and girls. By advocating for education, Malala is also challenging the social norms and cultural practices that perpetuate gender discrimination and inequality. Her work emphasizes the importance of creating an inclusive and equitable society where every girl has the opportunity to reach her full potential.

Malala's story has inspired numerous campaigns and initiatives aimed at promoting girls' education. Governments, international organizations, and civil society groups have responded to her call by increasing their efforts to ensure that girls have access to quality education. Malala's influence has also extended to the realm of policy-making, with several countries implementing reforms to improve girls' education and address the barriers they face.

Despite the progress made, Malala continues to remind the world that there is still much work to be done. Millions of girls around the world remain out of school due to factors such as poverty, conflict, and cultural norms. Malala's advocacy underscores the need for sustained and coordinated efforts to address these challenges and ensure that every girl has the opportunity to receive an education. Her work serves as a reminder of the ongoing struggle for girls' education and the importance of global solidarity in achieving this goal.

Malala's influence extends beyond her advocacy for education. She has become a symbol of resilience, courage, and the power of youth activism. Her story has inspired a new generation of young activists who are using their voices to advocate for social change. Malala's ability to connect with young people and her message of hope and empowerment have made her a role model for youth around the world. Her journey from a young girl in Pakistan to a global advocate for education demonstrates the potential of young people to make a difference.

Malala's impact is also reflected in the numerous awards and honors she has received. In addition to the Nobel Peace Prize, she has been awarded the Sakharov Prize for Freedom of Thought, the United Nations Human Rights Prize, and honorary Canadian citizenship, among others. These accolades recognize her contributions to the fight for education and human rights and serve as a testament to the significance of her work.

Malala's personal journey and advocacy have also been the subject of documentaries, films, and other media projects. The 2015 documentary "He Named Me Malala" provides an intimate look at her life, her family, and her activism. Through these portrayals, Malala's message reaches a wider audience, raising awareness about the importance of education and the challenges faced by girls around the world.

As Malala continues her studies at the University of Oxford, she remains committed to her mission of advocating for girls' education. Her academic pursuits reflect her belief in the importance of education and her desire to continue learning and growing as an advocate. Malala's ability to balance her studies with her activism is a testament to her dedication and passion for the cause.

Malala Yousafzai's story is a powerful reminder of the importance of education and the impact it can have on individuals and communities. Her unwavering commitment to advocating for girls' education, despite the risks and challenges she has faced, has made her a global symbol of hope and resilience. Malala's work with the Malala Fund and her continued advocacy serve as a beacon of light for millions of girls who are still fighting for their right to learn.

In conclusion, Malala Yousafzai's cry for education is a call to action for the global community to ensure that every girl has the opportunity to receive a quality education. Her story highlights the transformative power of education and the importance of empowering girls to reach their full potential. Malala's journey from the Swat Valley to the global stage is a testament to the strength of the human spirit and the ability of one individual to make a difference. Her legacy will continue to inspire and guide the fight for education and equality for years to come.

ᗪᗪᗪ

"As the sun rises with the dawn of each new day, so too does the opportunity for growth and renewal, beckoning us to embrace the limitless potential of the present moment."

SIX

MARGARET THATCHER: THE IRON LADY'S RESOLVE

Margaret Thatcher, often referred to as the Iron Lady, was a figure of immense political influence and resolve. As the first female Prime Minister of the United Kingdom, she served from 1979 to 1990, making her the longest-serving British prime minister of the 20th century. Her tenure was marked by significant economic, social, and political changes, many of which were deeply controversial. Thatcher's resolve, her unyielding commitment to her policies, and her distinctive leadership style have left an enduring legacy that continues to shape British politics and global economic thought.

Born on October 13, 1925, in Grantham, Lincolnshire, Margaret Hilda Roberts was the daughter of a grocer and a dressmaker. Her upbringing in a modest, hardworking family instilled in her a strong work ethic and conservative values. She excelled academically, earning a scholarship to study chemistry at Somerville College, Oxford. After graduating, she worked briefly as a research chemist before turning her attention to law and politics. Thatcher's early political career was characterized by her determination and perseverance, traits that would define her leadership style.

Thatcher entered politics at a time when Britain was grappling with economic challenges and a declining global influence. The post-war consensus, characterized by a mixed economy and a strong welfare state, was being increasingly questioned. Thatcher's ascent within the Conservative Party was driven by her conviction that radical changes were necessary to revive the British economy. She became the leader of the Conservative Party in 1975 and, four years later, led her party to a decisive victory in the general election, becoming Prime Minister.

One of Thatcher's core beliefs was the importance of reducing the role of the state in the economy. She was a staunch advocate of free-market principles, privatization, deregulation, and reducing the power of trade unions. Her economic policies, often referred to as Thatcherism, sought to curb inflation, reduce public expenditure, and foster individual entrepreneurship. One of her first major economic moves was to tackle inflation through tight monetary policies. This decision, while effective in reducing inflation, also led to a period of recession and high unemployment, drawing significant criticism.

Thatcher's commitment to privatization was one of the hallmarks of her tenure. She believed that state-owned industries were inefficient and that privatization would lead to increased competition, efficiency, and consumer choice. Her government privatized several major industries, including British Telecom, British Gas, and British Airways. This shift fundamentally transformed the British economy, creating a shareholder society and altering the relationship between the state and the market. While privatization generated substantial revenue for the government and was seen as a success in many quarters, it also led to job losses and criticism over the social implications of selling public assets.

Thatcher's resolve was perhaps most famously tested during the miners' strike of 1984-1985. The National Union of Mineworkers (NUM), led by Arthur Scargill, called a strike in response to planned pit closures, which threatened thousands of jobs. Thatcher's government was determined to resist the strike, viewing it as a challenge to her economic reforms and her authority. The strike lasted for a year and was marked by intense and often violent confrontations between miners and the police. Thatcher's refusal to back down, despite widespread public unrest and the economic impact, demonstrated her iron resolve. The strike ultimately ended in defeat for the NUM, significantly weakening the power of trade unions in Britain and reinforcing Thatcher's reputation as a formidable leader.

In foreign policy, Thatcher's tenure was marked by a strong alignment with the United States and a firm stance against the Soviet Union during the Cold War. Her relationship with U.S. President Ronald Reagan was particularly notable; both leaders shared a commitment to free-market principles and a hardline approach to communism. Thatcher's resolve in foreign policy was perhaps most dramatically demonstrated during the Falklands War in 1982. When Argentina invaded the Falkland Islands, a British territory in the South Atlantic, Thatcher ordered a task force to retake the islands. The successful military campaign boosted her popularity at home and reinforced her image as a determined and decisive leader.

Thatcher's approach to European integration was complex and often contentious. While she supported Britain's membership in the European Economic Community (EEC), she was skeptical of moves towards deeper political integration. Her famous Bruges speech in

1988 outlined her vision of a Europe of sovereign states cooperating economically but retaining their national identities. She opposed the idea of a federal Europe and was critical of what she saw as the centralization of power in Brussels. Thatcher's stance on Europe created tensions within her own party and among European leaders, but it also laid the groundwork for the eurosceptic movement within British politics.

Socially, Thatcher's policies were aimed at promoting individual responsibility and reducing dependence on the state. She introduced measures to encourage home ownership, such as the Right to Buy scheme, which allowed tenants in public housing to purchase their homes at discounted rates. This policy was popular and led to a significant increase in home ownership, but it also reduced the availability of social housing and contributed to long-term housing shortages. Thatcher's government also reformed the welfare system, aiming to reduce benefits and encourage self-reliance. Critics argued that these policies increased inequality and social division, while supporters claimed they promoted economic independence and personal initiative.

Thatcher's leadership style was characterized by her directness, clarity of purpose, and willingness to take bold decisions. She was known for her forthright manner and her ability to articulate her vision with conviction. Her speeches often emphasized themes of individual freedom, economic liberalism, and national pride. One of her most famous quotes, "There is no such thing as society. There are individual men and women, and there are families," encapsulated her belief in personal responsibility and the limits of state intervention. This philosophy underpinned much of her domestic policy agenda and resonated with many voters, particularly those who felt disenfranchised by the post-war consensus.

However, Thatcher's uncompromising style also alienated many within her own party and beyond. Her refusal to bend on key issues and her centralization of power created tensions with colleagues and opponents alike. These internal divisions came to a head over the issue of the Community Charge, commonly known as the poll tax. Introduced in 1990, the poll tax was a flat-rate local tax that replaced the existing system of rates based on property values. The policy was deeply unpopular, leading to widespread protests and riots. The backlash against the poll tax, combined with growing dissent within the Conservative Party, ultimately led to Thatcher's resignation in November 1990.

Thatcher's departure from office marked the end of an era, but her influence on British politics and economic policy remained profound. Her legacy is complex and contested, reflecting the transformative but divisive nature of her leadership. Supporters credit her with revitalizing the British economy, curbing the power of trade unions, and restoring national confidence. They argue that her policies laid the foundation for a more dynamic and competitive economy, fostering entrepreneurship and innovation. Critics, however, contend that her policies increased inequality, eroded social cohesion, and dismantled essential public services. They highlight the social costs of her economic reforms and the enduring impact on communities affected by industrial decline.

In the years following her resignation, Thatcher remained an influential figure in British politics and a vocal advocate for her ideas. She published her memoirs, "The Downing Street Years" and "The Path to Power," which provided insights into her time in office and her political philosophy. Thatcher continued to speak on issues such as European integration and economic policy, reinforcing her views on the importance of national sovereignty and free markets. Her legacy continued to shape the Conservative Party, with subsequent leaders grappling with the balance between upholding her principles and adapting to changing political realities.

Thatcher's death on April 8, 2013, prompted a national and

international reflection on her life and legacy. Tributes poured in from world leaders, highlighting her role in ending the Cold War, her partnership with Reagan, and her impact on global economic policy. At the same time, her passing rekindled debates about the social and economic consequences of her tenure. Public reactions ranged from admiration and respect to protest and criticism, underscoring the enduring polarization surrounding her legacy.

Margaret Thatcher's resolve and her impact on British and global politics remain subjects of study and debate. Her leadership exemplified the power of conviction and the ability to implement radical change in the face of opposition. Thatcher's policies and principles continue to influence political discourse, shaping debates on economic policy, state intervention, and the role of government in society. Her tenure serves as a case study in the complexities of leadership, the challenges of implementing transformative policies, and the enduring tension between economic efficiency and social equity.

In conclusion, Margaret Thatcher's tenure as Prime Minister was marked by her unwavering resolve and her commitment to transforming the British economy and society. Her advocacy for free-market principles, privatization, and reduced state intervention fundamentally altered the course of British politics. While her policies and leadership style were deeply divisive, they also demonstrated the power of steadfast conviction and the potential for political leaders to effect significant change. Thatcher's legacy is a testament to her influence and a reminder of the enduring debates over the balance between economic liberalism and social responsibility.

ᐳᐳᐳ

"Life's journey is a mosaic of moments, each piece
intricately crafted from the tapestry of our
experiences, forming a masterpiece of memories
that define our essence."

SEVEN

ANGELA MERKEL: LEADERSHIP IN CRISIS

Angela Merkel's tenure as Chancellor of Germany has been marked by her steadfast leadership, particularly during times of crisis. Throughout her time in office, Merkel has navigated numerous challenges, both domestically and internationally, with a pragmatic and steady approach that has earned her respect on the global stage. From economic downturns to refugee crises, Merkel's leadership style has been characterized by her ability to maintain stability and consensus in the face of adversity.

One of the most notable instances of Merkel's leadership in crisis occurred during the global financial crisis of 2008. As the leader of Europe's largest economy, Merkel faced immense pressure to steer Germany through the economic downturn and prevent the collapse of the Eurozone. Merkel's response was characterized by a combination of fiscal discipline and targeted stimulus measures aimed at stabilizing the economy while safeguarding the interests of German taxpayers. Her pragmatic approach helped Germany emerge from the crisis relatively unscathed compared to many of its

European counterparts.

Another significant challenge Merkel faced was the European sovereign debt crisis that unfolded in the early 2010s. Once again, Merkel found herself at the center of efforts to address the crisis and prevent it from spreading further within the Eurozone. Despite facing criticism from some quarters for her handling of the crisis, Merkel remained resolute in her commitment to fiscal responsibility and structural reforms. Her leadership was instrumental in securing bailout packages for struggling economies like Greece and Portugal, albeit with strict conditions attached.

Merkel's leadership was put to the test once again during the refugee crisis of 2015. Faced with an unprecedented influx of refugees fleeing conflict and persecution in the Middle East and North Africa, Merkel made the controversial decision to open Germany's borders to those seeking asylum. While her decision was met with both praise and criticism, Merkel remained steadfast in her conviction that Germany had a moral obligation to provide refuge to those in need. Despite facing domestic political backlash and challenges in managing the influx of migrants, Merkel's leadership during the crisis was guided by compassion and a commitment to upholding humanitarian values.

In addition to her handling of economic and humanitarian crises, Merkel has also demonstrated strong leadership on the international stage. As one of the most influential leaders in the European Union, Merkel has played a key role in shaping EU policies and initiatives, particularly in the areas of foreign policy and security. Merkel's diplomatic skills and ability to build consensus have been evident in her efforts to address issues such as Brexit, the conflict in Ukraine, and tensions with Russia.

Furthermore, Merkel has been a vocal advocate for multilateralism and international cooperation, particularly in the face of growing global challenges such as climate change and the COVID-19 pandemic. Throughout her tenure as Chancellor, Merkel has consistently emphasized the importance of dialogue and collaboration in addressing complex global issues. Her leadership in advocating for the Paris Agreement on climate change and her role in coordinating the European response to the COVID-19 pandemic have underscored her commitment to multilateralism and solidarity.

However, Merkel's leadership has not been without its criticisms. Some have accused her of being too cautious and incremental in her approach to policy-making, particularly on issues such as economic reform and European integration. Others have criticized her for what they perceive as a lack of bold vision and leadership on certain issues. Nonetheless, Merkel's ability to maintain stability and consensus in Germany and Europe has earned her widespread respect and admiration, both at home and abroad.

As Merkel prepares to step down from office after 16 years as Chancellor, her legacy as a leader in crisis will undoubtedly be remembered. Whether navigating economic downturns, refugee crises, or global pandemics, Merkel has consistently demonstrated resilience, pragmatism, and compassion in her leadership. While her tenure has not been without its challenges and criticisms, Merkel's steady hand and commitment to upholding democratic values have left an indelible mark on Germany and the world. As she passes the baton to her successor, Merkel leaves behind a legacy of leadership in crisis that will continue to inspire future generations of leaders.

ᐳᐳᐳ

"Embrace the dance of impermanence, for in the rhythm of change lies the melody of growth, orchestrating the symphony of our evolution with grace and resilience."

EIGHT

AUNG SAN SUU KYI: THE QUEST FOR DEMOCRACY

Aung San Suu Kyi's life and work have been emblematic of the struggle for democracy and human rights in Myanmar, formerly known as Burma. Her quest for democracy has been marked by immense personal sacrifice, political turmoil, and an unwavering commitment to her country's future. Born on June 19, 1945, in Rangoon (now Yangon), Aung San Suu Kyi is the daughter of Aung San, a revered leader who played a crucial role in Burma's fight for independence from British rule. Her mother, Khin Kyi, was also a prominent figure in Burmese politics and diplomacy, serving as Burma's ambassador to India and Nepal.

Aung San Suu Kyi's early years were shaped by the legacy of her father, who was assassinated in 1947 when she was just two years old. Her father's vision of a free and democratic Burma deeply influenced her worldview. Suu Kyi was educated in Burma, India, and later at the University of Oxford in the United Kingdom, where she studied philosophy, politics, and economics. Her time abroad exposed her to democratic ideals and further solidified her belief in the importance of freedom and human rights.

In 1988, Aung San Suu Kyi returned to Burma to care for her ailing mother. Her return coincided with a period of significant political upheaval. The country was under the oppressive rule of a military junta, and widespread pro-democracy protests were erupting across the nation. These protests, known as the 8888 Uprising, saw thousands of Burmese citizens, including students, monks, and ordinary civilians, taking to the streets to demand democratic reforms and an end to military rule. The military responded with brutal force, resulting in the deaths of thousands of protesters.

Amid this turmoil, Aung San Suu Kyi emerged as a prominent leader of the pro-democracy movement. Drawing on her father's legacy and her own convictions, she co-founded the National League for Democracy (NLD) and began advocating for nonviolent resistance and political reform. Her speeches and public appearances galvanized the movement, and she quickly became a symbol of hope and resilience for the Burmese people. Suu Kyi's calls for democracy, human rights, and the rule of law resonated with a population yearning for change.

In 1990, the military junta allowed multiparty elections, which the NLD won by a landslide, securing over 80% of the parliamentary seats. However, the junta refused to recognize the results and continued to cling to power. Aung San Suu Kyi was placed under house arrest, a confinement that would last, intermittently, for 15 of the next 21 years. During her periods of house arrest, she remained a steadfast advocate for democracy, using her confinement to write and communicate with the outside world. Her writings, including the collection of essays "Freedom from Fear," articulated her vision for a democratic Burma and the principles of nonviolence and justice.

Aung San Suu Kyi's struggle and perseverance earned her

international acclaim and numerous accolades, including the Nobel Peace Prize in 1991. The Nobel Committee recognized her "nonviolent struggle for democracy and human rights" and highlighted her role as "one of the most extraordinary examples of civil courage in Asia in recent decades." The award brought global attention to the plight of the Burmese people and the oppressive nature of the military regime. It also intensified international pressure on the junta to release her and move towards democratic reforms.

Throughout her years of house arrest, Suu Kyi's commitment to nonviolence and dialogue remained unwavering. She drew inspiration from Mahatma Gandhi and Martin Luther King Jr., embracing their philosophies of peaceful resistance and moral integrity. Her leadership style emphasized the power of ethical principles and the importance of remaining steadfast in the face of adversity. Suu Kyi's ability to endure personal hardship while maintaining her dedication to the cause of democracy earned her widespread admiration and support both domestically and internationally.

The political landscape in Myanmar began to shift in the late 2000s and early 2010s. In 2010, the military junta initiated a series of political reforms, ostensibly aimed at transitioning towards a civilian government. As part of these reforms, Aung San Suu Kyi was released from house arrest in November 2010. Her release was met with jubilation by her supporters and the international community. She immediately resumed her political activities, continuing to advocate for democratic change and participating in the political process.

In 2012, the NLD contested by-elections, and Aung San Suu Kyi won a seat in the Pyithu Hluttaw, the lower house of Myanmar's parliament. This marked a significant milestone in her political journey and symbolized a shift towards greater political openness in the country. Her presence in parliament provided a platform to push for further reforms and to hold the government accountable. Suu Kyi's participation in the political process was seen as a hopeful sign of Myanmar's gradual transition towards democracy.

The watershed moment in Aung San Suu Kyi's political career came in the 2015 general elections. The NLD won a decisive victory, securing a majority in both houses of parliament. Although the military retained significant power through a constitution that reserved key government positions and parliamentary seats for military officials, the election was a clear mandate for democratic change. Aung San Suu Kyi, unable to become president due to a constitutional provision that barred her from holding the office, assumed the role of State Counsellor, a position created for her that allowed her to effectively lead the government.

As State Counsellor, Aung San Suu Kyi faced numerous challenges. The legacy of decades of military rule, economic underdevelopment, and ethnic conflicts presented significant obstacles to her administration. Her government embarked on efforts to implement democratic reforms, promote economic development, and address the country's myriad social and political issues. However, the limitations imposed by the military's continued influence and the complexity of Myanmar's internal dynamics posed substantial challenges.

One of the most significant and controversial issues during Aung San Suu Kyi's tenure was the treatment of the Rohingya Muslim minority. In 2017, a military crackdown in Rakhine State led to widespread violence, mass displacement, and allegations of atrocities, including ethnic cleansing and genocide. Hundreds of thousands of Rohingya fled to neighboring Bangladesh, creating a humanitarian crisis. The international community criticized Aung San Suu Kyi for her perceived failure to condemn the military's actions and protect the Rohingya. Her response to the crisis strained her international standing and called into question her commitment to human rights.

Supporters of Aung San Suu Kyi argued that her position was constrained by the political realities in Myanmar, where the military retained significant power and autonomy. They contended that open confrontation with the military could destabilize the country and jeopardize the fragile democratic transition. Critics, however, argued that her silence and reluctance to address the abuses against the Rohingya represented a betrayal of the principles of human rights and justice that she had long championed.

Despite these controversies, Aung San Suu Kyi remained a central figure in Myanmar's political landscape. Her quest for democracy continued to be driven by a deep-seated belief in the importance of freedom, justice, and the rule of law. She sought to balance the demands of governance with the need to navigate the complex and often fraught relationship with the military. Her leadership emphasized the importance of patience, pragmatism, and resilience in the face of formidable challenges.

In 2020, the NLD once again secured a landslide victory in the general elections, reaffirming the public's support for Aung San Suu Kyi and her party. However, the military disputed the election results, alleging widespread fraud, and on February 1, 2021, they staged a coup, detaining Aung San Suu Kyi and other NLD leaders. The coup sparked widespread protests and a civil disobedience movement, with citizens demanding the restoration of democracy and the release of their elected leaders. The military's response was marked by brutal crackdowns, leading to numerous casualties and a deepening political crisis.

The coup and subsequent events underscored the fragility of Myanmar's democratic transition and the persistent challenges posed by the military's entrenched power. Aung San Suu Kyi's detention once again highlighted her role as a symbol of resistance and the enduring struggle for democracy in Myanmar. The international community condemned the coup and called for the restoration of civilian rule, while supporters of Aung San Suu Kyi continued to rally for her release and the resumption of the democratic process.

Aung San Suu Kyi's quest for democracy in Myanmar is a story of remarkable courage, resilience, and unwavering commitment to the principles of freedom and justice. Her leadership has been characterized by her ability to inspire and mobilize the Burmese people, her dedication to nonviolence and dialogue, and her willingness to endure personal sacrifice for the greater good. Despite the numerous challenges and setbacks she has faced, Aung San Suu Kyi's vision for a democratic Myanmar remains a guiding light for many.

Her legacy is complex and multifaceted, reflecting both her significant contributions to the pro-democracy movement and the controversies that have arisen during her political career. Aung San Suu Kyi's story is a testament to the enduring power of principled leadership and the importance of standing firm in the face of oppression. As Myanmar continues to navigate its path towards democracy, her role as a symbol of resistance and hope will remain a crucial part of the nation's history and its ongoing struggle for freedom and human rights.

In conclusion, Aung San Suu Kyi's quest for democracy in Myanmar has been marked by immense challenges, personal sacrifices, and significant achievements. Her unwavering commitment to democratic principles and human rights has inspired countless individuals both within Myanmar and around the world. Despite the controversies and setbacks, her legacy as a champion of democracy and a symbol of resilience endures. As Myanmar faces the future, the ideals and vision that Aung San Su

❦❦❦

"Like a phoenix rising from the ashes, our spirits soar on the wings of resilience, fueled by the fire of determination to conquer the challenges that lie ahead."

NINE

MICHELLE OBAMA: EMPOWERING THE NEXT GENERATION

Michelle Obama's influence as a public figure, advocate, and role model has been profoundly impactful, particularly in empowering the next generation. Her journey from a working-class upbringing on the South Side of Chicago to becoming the first African American First Lady of the United States is a story of determination, resilience, and a deep commitment to public service. Throughout her time in the White House and beyond, Michelle Obama has used her platform to champion education, health, and empowerment, inspiring millions of young people to reach their full potential.

Born on January 17, 1964, Michelle LaVaughn Robinson was raised in a close-knit family that valued education and hard work. Her parents, Fraser and Marian Robinson, instilled in her the importance of striving for excellence and making the most of every opportunity. Despite facing the challenges of growing up in a racially segregated society, Michelle excelled academically, earning a place at Princeton University and later attending Harvard Law School. Her educational achievements laid the foundation for her future career and advocacy work.

Michelle's professional journey began in law, where she worked at the prestigious Sidley & Austin law firm in Chicago. It was there that she met Barack Obama, who would later become her husband and the 44th President of the United States. Her career path shifted towards public service, reflecting her desire to make a tangible difference in her community. She worked for the Chicago city government and later for the University of Chicago, focusing on community outreach and education.

As First Lady from 2009 to 2017, Michelle Obama redefined the role by actively engaging in initiatives that addressed critical issues facing the nation. One of her most significant contributions was her focus on education, particularly for girls and underserved communities. She launched the "Let Girls Learn" initiative in 2015, aimed at addressing the barriers that prevent millions of girls around the world from receiving an education. This initiative emphasized the importance of education in empowering girls to achieve their dreams and contribute to their communities.

Michelle's advocacy for education extended to the United States through her "Reach Higher" initiative, which encouraged young people to pursue higher education and career training. She emphasized the importance of college accessibility and readiness, providing resources and support to help students navigate the college application process. Her efforts were particularly focused on first-generation college students and those from low-income backgrounds, ensuring that all young people had the opportunity to succeed regardless of their circumstances.

Michelle Obama's approach to empowerment was holistic, recognizing that education alone was not enough. She also championed health and wellness through her "Let's Move!" initiative, which aimed to combat childhood obesity and promote healthy lifestyles. Launched in 2010, "Let's Move!" encouraged physical activity, healthy eating, and nutritional education. Michelle's efforts included working with schools to improve lunch programs, encouraging physical activity, and advocating for better food labeling. Her commitment to health and wellness highlighted the connection between physical well-being and the ability to achieve academic and personal success.

Michelle Obama's influence extended beyond policy initiatives to her ability to connect with people on a personal level. Her authenticity, relatability, and ability to share her own experiences resonated deeply with many. She used her platform to speak openly about her own challenges, including balancing work and family, dealing with public scrutiny, and navigating the pressures of being in the public eye. By sharing her story, she provided a source of inspiration and encouragement to those facing similar struggles.

One of the defining moments of Michelle Obama's tenure as First Lady was her speech at the Democratic National Convention in 2016. Her eloquence and passion were evident as she spoke about the importance of role models and the impact of words and actions on children. Her phrase "When they go low, we go high" became a rallying cry for civility, integrity, and perseverance. This speech encapsulated her belief in the power of positive influence and the responsibility of leaders to set an example for the next generation.

After leaving the White House, Michelle Obama continued her advocacy work and broadened her impact through various projects and initiatives. Her memoir, "Becoming," published in 2018, offered an intimate look at her life, from her childhood to her experiences as First Lady. The book became a bestseller and was praised for its honesty, insight, and inspirational message. In "Becoming," Michelle shared her journey of self-discovery, the challenges she faced, and the lessons she learned along the way. The memoir provided readers with a deeper understanding of her values, motivations, and aspirations, reinforcing her role as a powerful advocate for empowerment and change.

In addition to her memoir, Michelle launched the "Becoming" book tour, which included conversations and discussions with diverse audiences around the world. These events provided a platform for her to engage directly with young people, share her experiences, and encourage them to pursue their dreams. Her ability to connect with audiences through storytelling and candid dialogue underscored her commitment to inspiring and empowering the next generation.

Michelle Obama's influence also extends to her work with the Obama Foundation, an organization dedicated to developing the next generation of leaders and promoting civic engagement. Through initiatives like the Obama Foundation Scholars Program and the Leaders program, the foundation provides resources, mentorship, and training to emerging leaders from around the world. Michelle's involvement in these programs reflects her belief in the importance of nurturing leadership and fostering a sense of civic responsibility among young people.

Another significant aspect of Michelle Obama's legacy is her commitment to gender equality and women's empowerment. She has consistently used her platform to advocate for the rights and opportunities of women and girls, both in the United States and globally. Her work with initiatives like Let Girls Learn and her support for organizations that promote gender equality highlight her dedication to addressing the systemic barriers that hinder women's progress. Michelle's advocacy emphasizes the importance of creating an inclusive society where all individuals have the opportunity to succeed, regardless of gender.

Michelle Obama's influence is also evident in her ability to inspire and mobilize people through her public speaking and media appearances. Her speeches, interviews, and participation in public events continue to resonate with diverse audiences, providing a source of motivation and encouragement. Her presence in popular culture, including her appearances on television shows and podcasts, allows her to reach a broad audience and share her message of empowerment and resilience.

One of the key themes in Michelle Obama's work is the importance of self-belief and perseverance. She often speaks about the challenges she faced growing up and the obstacles she overcame to achieve her goals. Her message emphasizes the power of education, hard work, and determination in overcoming adversity and achieving success. By sharing her own journey, Michelle provides a powerful example of what is possible when individuals believe in themselves and work towards their dreams.

Michelle Obama's impact on young people is further amplified by her engagement with social media and digital platforms. Through her social media presence, she connects with millions of followers, sharing messages of encouragement, inspiration, and advocacy. Her use of digital platforms allows her to engage with a global audience, providing a space for dialogue and connection. Michelle's ability to leverage technology to amplify her message highlights her adaptability and commitment to reaching and empowering the next generation.

In addition to her individual efforts, Michelle Obama's partnership with Barack Obama has also been a source of inspiration for many. Together, they have demonstrated the power of teamwork, mutual support, and shared values in achieving their goals. Their partnership has been a model of collaboration and commitment, both in their public roles and in their personal lives. Michelle and Barack's joint initiatives, such as the Obama Foundation, reflect their shared vision of empowering future leaders and promoting social change.

Michelle Obama's influence extends beyond her time in the White House, leaving a lasting legacy that continues to inspire and empower individuals around the world. Her dedication to education, health, gender equality, and leadership development has had a profound impact on countless lives. Through her initiatives, public speaking, and personal story, she has provided a powerful example of what is possible when individuals are empowered to reach their full potential.

In conclusion, Michelle Obama's commitment to empowering the next generation has been a defining aspect of her public life and legacy. Her advocacy for education, health, and gender equality, combined with her ability to connect with people on a personal level, has inspired millions to pursue their dreams and make a positive impact in their communities. Michelle's journey from the South Side of Chicago to the global stage is a testament to the power of resilience, determination, and the belief in the potential of every individual. Her work continues to shape and inspire future generations, leaving an indelible mark on the world.

"In the vast expanse of time, our lives are but fleeting moments, yet within each heartbeat lies the potential to ignite the flame of resilience, illuminating the path to greatness."

TEN

GRETA THUNBERG: THE VOICE OF CLIMATE CHANGE

Greta Thunberg, a name that has become synonymous with the climate change movement, emerged as a leading voice for environmental activism at an extraordinarily young age. Born on January 3, 2003, in Stockholm, Sweden, Greta's journey to becoming an international figure began with a personal awakening about the dire state of the planet. Her story is one of unwavering determination, resilience, and the power of youth to effect global change. Greta's activism has brought unprecedented attention to the climate crisis, galvanized millions of young people, and pressured world leaders to take more decisive action on climate change.

Greta's awareness of climate change began at the age of eight when she first learned about global warming and its consequences. The more she learned, the more she became distressed about the lack of significant action being taken to address the crisis. Greta was diagnosed with Asperger syndrome, obsessive-compulsive disorder (OCD), and selective mutism. While these conditions presented challenges, Greta has often described them as giving her a different perspective, allowing her to focus intensely on the climate crisis and speak out with clarity and urgency.

In August 2018, at the age of 15, Greta began her solo climate strike outside the Swedish Parliament. Holding a sign that read "Skolstrejk för klimatet" (School Strike for Climate), she skipped school every Friday to protest the lack of action on climate change. This act of defiance quickly captured the attention of the media and resonated with students and activists around the world. Greta's school strike for climate sparked the "Fridays for Future" movement, inspiring students globally to join her in striking from school to demand urgent climate action.

Greta's activism is characterized by her direct, unapologetic communication style. She has repeatedly called out world leaders for their inaction and hypocrisy regarding climate change. Her speeches are marked by their stark honesty and powerful rhetoric, often highlighting the gap between political promises and actual policies. In her famous address to the United Nations Climate Change Conference (COP24) in December 2018, Greta declared, "You are not mature enough to tell it like it is. Even that burden you leave to us children." Her words underscored the frustration of her generation, who will bear the brunt of climate change's impacts if immediate action is not taken.

One of Greta's most impactful speeches was delivered at the United Nations Climate Action Summit in September 2019. With palpable anger and emotion, she scolded world leaders, saying, "How dare you! You have stolen my dreams and my childhood with your empty words." She criticized them for their failure to act decisively and for treating the climate crisis as a problem for the future, rather than an immediate emergency. Her speech was a wake-up call, amplifying the urgency of the climate crisis and emphasizing the moral responsibility of those in power to protect the planet for future generations.

Greta's activism is not just about speeches and protests; it is also deeply rooted in scientific understanding. She has consistently emphasized the importance of listening to scientists and basing policies on scientific evidence. Greta's ability to distill complex scientific data into compelling messages has been a key factor in her effectiveness as an activist. She often quotes reports from the Intergovernmental Panel on Climate Change (IPCC) and other scientific bodies to highlight the urgency of the crisis and the need for immediate action.

The impact of Greta Thunberg's activism has been profound. Her school strike movement grew into a global phenomenon, with millions of students participating in climate strikes around the world. These strikes have brought unprecedented attention to the climate crisis and have put pressure on governments and corporations to take meaningful action. Greta's influence has also extended to the political sphere, where she has met with numerous world leaders and addressed various legislative bodies, including the European Parliament and the US Congress. In these forums, she has consistently called for policymakers to enact bold climate policies that align with the scientific consensus.

Greta's activism has also highlighted the intergenerational aspect of the climate crisis. She has repeatedly pointed out that young people will suffer the most from the effects of climate change, despite having the least responsibility for causing it. This perspective has galvanized youth around the world, who see in Greta a relatable and inspiring figure. The youth-led nature of the climate movement has brought new energy and urgency to the fight against climate change, challenging the status quo and demanding more ambitious action.

Greta's impact is also evident in the media. She has been featured in countless news articles, documentaries, and interviews, bringing widespread attention to the climate crisis. Her image has become iconic, symbolizing the power of individual action and the importance of speaking truth to power. Greta has used her platform to amplify the voices of other young activists and marginalized communities who are disproportionately affected by climate change. Her emphasis on inclusivity and solidarity has strengthened the global climate movement, making it more diverse and representative.

In addition to her public activism, Greta has also taken practical steps to reduce her own carbon footprint. She famously sailed across the Atlantic Ocean in a zero-emissions yacht to attend the UN Climate Action Summit in New York, avoiding the emissions associated with air travel. This journey was not only a personal statement but also a demonstration of her commitment to living her values. Greta's actions have inspired many to consider their own environmental impact and to take steps to reduce their carbon footprints.

Greta Thunberg's activism has not been without challenges and criticism. She has faced backlash from climate change deniers, political opponents, and even some members of the media. Critics have accused her of being alarmist, questioned her understanding of complex issues, and attacked her personally. Despite this, Greta has remained resolute and focused on her mission. She has continued to speak out, undeterred by the criticism, and has used it as further motivation to push for change.

Greta's influence has been recognized through numerous awards and honors. She was named Time magazine's Person of the Year in 2019, making her the youngest person ever to receive the accolade. She has also been nominated for the Nobel Peace Prize multiple times and has received various environmental and humanitarian awards. These recognitions reflect her significant impact on raising awareness about the climate crisis and mobilizing global action.

Greta's story is a powerful example of how one individual can make a difference. Her journey from a solitary school strike to leading a global movement demonstrates the power of conviction, courage, and persistence. Greta's ability to inspire and mobilize people around the world has shown that collective action is possible and that young people have a crucial role to play in shaping the future.

Looking ahead, Greta Thunberg continues to be a prominent voice in the fight against climate change. She remains committed to holding leaders accountable and pushing for policies that will ensure a sustainable and just future. Greta's work highlights the importance of continued advocacy, education, and action in addressing the climate crisis. Her emphasis on listening to science and prioritizing the well-being of future generations serves as a guiding principle for the movement.

In conclusion, Greta Thunberg has become the voice of climate change through her passionate advocacy, unwavering commitment, and ability to mobilize millions. Her journey from a solitary protester to a global icon illustrates the power of individual action and the importance of speaking out for what one believes in. Greta's influence has brought unprecedented attention to the climate crisis, galvanized youth activism, and pressured world leaders to take more decisive action. Her legacy is one of courage, resilience, and hope, inspiring a new generation to fight for a sustainable and just future.

ppp

"The winds of adversity may howl and the storms
of life may rage, but within the shelter of our souls
lies the calm resilience that guides us through the
tempest."

ELEVEN

JACINDA ARDERN: COMPASSIONATE LEADERSHIP

Jacinda Ardern's rise to global prominence as the Prime Minister of New Zealand is a remarkable story of compassionate leadership in the modern political landscape. Born on July 26, 1980, in Hamilton, New Zealand, Ardern's journey into politics began at a young age, influenced by her family's active engagement in their community and her exposure to social justice issues. Her political career, marked by a rapid ascent through the ranks of the Labour Party, ultimately led her to become one of the world's youngest female heads of government. Ardern's leadership style, characterized by empathy, inclusiveness, and a strong moral compass, has set her apart and garnered international acclaim.

Ardern's early life was shaped by her upbringing in a modest, working-class family. Her father, Ross Ardern, was a police officer, and her mother, Laurell Ardern, worked as a school catering assistant. These experiences instilled in her a deep sense of empathy and a commitment to social justice. Ardern's political career began while she was still a student at the University of Waikato, where she studied communications and political science. Her involvement with the Labour Party started at the grassroots level, and she quickly rose through the ranks due to her passion, dedication, and effective communication skills.

After graduating, Ardern worked as a researcher in the office of Prime Minister Helen Clark, one of her early mentors. She then moved to London, where she served as a policy advisor in the Cabinet Office under Tony Blair's administration. These experiences broadened her understanding of politics and governance, and she returned to New Zealand with a renewed commitment to public service. In 2008, at the age of 28, Ardern was elected as a Member of Parliament for the Labour Party.

Ardern's rise to the leadership of the Labour Party was swift and unexpected. In August 2017, just weeks before the general election, she was appointed as the party's leader following the resignation of Andrew Little. Despite the short timeframe, Ardern energized the Labour Party's campaign with her charisma, optimism, and a clear vision for New Zealand's future. Her ability to connect with voters on a personal level and articulate a message of hope and change led to a surge in support, which became known as "Jacindamania."

In the 2017 general election, the Labour Party formed a coalition government with the New Zealand First Party and the Green Party, and Ardern became the Prime Minister. Her leadership style, often described as compassionate and inclusive, was immediately evident. Ardern emphasized the importance of addressing social inequalities, improving public services, and tackling environmental issues. Her government's policy agenda focused on child poverty reduction, mental health support, affordable housing, and climate change action.

One of the most defining moments of Ardern's leadership came in the aftermath of the Christchurch mosque shootings on March 15,

2019. A white supremacist gunman attacked two mosques, killing 51 people and injuring dozens more. The tragedy shocked the nation and the world. Ardern's response to the attack was characterized by her empathy, compassion, and decisive action. She quickly reached out to the Muslim community, offering comfort and solidarity. Her image, wearing a hijab and embracing grieving families, became a powerful symbol of unity and compassion.

Ardern's leadership extended beyond words. She moved swiftly to enact gun control legislation, banning semi-automatic weapons and implementing a gun buyback program. Her ability to navigate the legislative process and achieve bipartisan support for the reforms demonstrated her effectiveness as a leader. Ardern's response to the Christchurch attack was widely praised for its empathy, decisiveness, and the sense of national unity it fostered.

Another significant aspect of Ardern's leadership has been her approach to the COVID-19 pandemic. New Zealand's response, under her guidance, has been considered one of the most effective in the world. Ardern implemented strict lockdown measures early in the pandemic, prioritizing public health and safety. Her clear communication, transparency, and reliance on scientific advice helped to build public trust and compliance with the measures. As a result, New Zealand was able to control the spread of the virus effectively, allowing for a relatively quick return to normalcy compared to other countries.

Ardern's leadership during the pandemic was marked by her ability to balance empathy with pragmatism. She regularly addressed the nation, providing updates and reassurance while acknowledging the sacrifices and hardships faced by the public. Her emphasis on the collective effort needed to combat the virus resonated with New Zealanders, reinforcing a sense of community and shared responsibility. Ardern's handling of the pandemic further solidified her reputation as a compassionate and capable leader.

Beyond crisis management, Ardern has been a vocal advocate for progressive social policies. Her government has made significant strides in areas such as mental health, education, and social welfare. In 2019, Ardern's administration introduced the Wellbeing Budget, which prioritized mental health services, child poverty reduction, and measures to support the Maori and Pasifika communities. The budget represented a shift towards measuring success not just by economic growth, but by the overall wellbeing of the population.

Ardern's commitment to addressing climate change has also been a key aspect of her leadership. She has championed policies aimed at reducing carbon emissions, transitioning to renewable energy, and protecting New Zealand's natural environment. In 2019, her government passed the Zero Carbon Act, which set a legal framework for New Zealand to achieve net-zero carbon emissions by 2050. Ardern has emphasized the importance of global cooperation in addressing climate change and has positioned New Zealand as a leader in environmental sustainability.

Ardern's leadership style is characterized by her authenticity, humility, and approachability. She often emphasizes the importance of kindness and empathy in politics, advocating for a more compassionate approach to governance. Ardern's ability to connect with people on a personal level has endeared her to many, both in New Zealand and internationally. Her open and relatable demeanor, combined with her strong moral convictions, have made her a role model for leaders and aspiring politicians around the world.

Despite her many successes, Ardern's leadership has not been without challenges and criticism. Some have questioned her government's ability to deliver on ambitious promises, particularly in areas such as housing and child poverty. The pace of progress on some issues has been slower than anticipated, and Ardern has faced scrutiny over her administration's handling of economic and social challenges. However, her commitment to transparency and accountability has helped to maintain public trust and support.

Ardern's leadership has also been shaped by her experiences as a young, female leader in a male-dominated political landscape. She has spoken openly about the challenges of balancing her role as Prime Minister with her responsibilities as a mother, highlighting the need for greater support for working parents and more inclusive workplaces. Ardern's decision to take maternity leave while in office was a groundbreaking moment, challenging traditional perceptions of leadership and demonstrating that it is possible to lead effectively while prioritizing family.

Ardern's influence extends beyond her policy achievements and crisis management. She has become a symbol of compassionate and progressive leadership, inspiring a new generation of leaders to prioritize empathy, inclusiveness, and social justice. Her emphasis on kindness and collective wellbeing has resonated with people around the world, challenging the often adversarial and divisive nature of contemporary politics. Ardern's leadership offers a model for how political leaders can navigate complex challenges with integrity, humility, and a commitment to the greater good.

In conclusion, Jacinda Ardern's leadership has been marked by her compassionate approach, her commitment to social justice, and her ability to navigate crises with empathy and decisiveness. Her response to the Christchurch mosque shootings, her management of the COVID-19 pandemic, and her advocacy for progressive policies have set her apart as a transformative leader. Ardern's emphasis on kindness, inclusiveness, and collective wellbeing offers a powerful example of how leadership can be both effective and compassionate. Her impact extends beyond New Zealand, inspiring leaders and citizens around the world to strive for a more just and equitable society. Ardern's legacy will be remembered for her ability to lead with empathy, to champion progressive change, and to inspire a new generation to prioritize compassion in their pursuit of a better world.

❦❦❦

"Through the labyrinth of life, let resilience be your compass, guiding you through the twists and turns with unwavering resolve and steadfast determination."

TWELVE

BENAZIR BHUTTO: A VISION FOR PAKISTAN

Benazir Bhutto's legacy as a political leader in Pakistan is marked by her vision for a democratic and progressive nation. Born on June 21, 1953, in Karachi, Benazir was the daughter of Zulfikar Ali Bhutto, a prominent political figure who served as both President and Prime Minister of Pakistan. Her early exposure to politics, combined with a Western education at Harvard University and the University of Oxford, shaped her political ideals and aspirations. Benazir Bhutto's journey to becoming the first female Prime Minister of a Muslim-majority country was fraught with challenges, but her determination and vision for Pakistan left an indelible mark on the nation's history.

Benazir's childhood and upbringing were steeped in the political environment of her family. Her father, Zulfikar Ali Bhutto, founded the Pakistan People's Party (PPP) and was a charismatic leader known for his socialist policies and advocacy for the poor. Benazir was deeply influenced by her father's vision for Pakistan and his commitment to democracy and social justice. Her education in the

United States and the United Kingdom further broadened her perspectives, exposing her to diverse political ideologies and strengthening her belief in democratic principles.

Tragedy struck the Bhutto family when Zulfikar Ali Bhutto was overthrown in a military coup led by General Zia-ul-Haq in 1977. Zulfikar was subsequently executed in 1979, a move widely regarded as politically motivated. Benazir and her family faced immense persecution under Zia's military regime. She was placed under house arrest multiple times and spent years in exile. These experiences of repression and injustice fueled Benazir's resolve to fight for democracy and the rule of law in Pakistan.

In 1986, Benazir Bhutto returned to Pakistan from exile to lead the PPP in its struggle against the military dictatorship. Her return was marked by massive public rallies and widespread support from the Pakistani populace, who viewed her as a symbol of resistance and hope. Benazir's charisma, eloquence, and ability to connect with people from all walks of life garnered her a substantial following. She promised to restore democracy, address poverty, and improve the status of women in Pakistan.

Benazir Bhutto's vision for Pakistan was rooted in her commitment to democracy, social justice, and economic development. She believed that democracy was essential for the nation's progress and stability. Her political philosophy was heavily influenced by her father's socialist ideals, emphasizing the need to address social inequalities and uplift the marginalized sections of society. Benazir was a strong advocate for women's rights and education, recognizing that empowering women was crucial for the country's overall development.

In 1988, Benazir Bhutto made history by becoming the first female Prime Minister of Pakistan and the first woman to lead a Muslim-majority country. Her election was a significant milestone, symbolizing a break from the patriarchal norms that had long dominated Pakistani politics. Benazir's leadership brought a renewed sense of optimism and hope for democratic governance. During her first term, she focused on several key areas, including economic reform, social welfare, and women's empowerment.

Benazir's government introduced policies aimed at stimulating economic growth and reducing poverty. She prioritized the expansion of healthcare and education services, recognizing their importance in improving the quality of life for Pakistanis. Her administration also launched initiatives to enhance the role of women in society, including measures to increase women's representation in government and promote gender equality in the workplace. Benazir's efforts to empower women and improve social services were significant steps towards achieving her vision of a more equitable and progressive Pakistan.

However, Benazir's tenure as Prime Minister was fraught with challenges. Her government faced allegations of corruption, mismanagement, and political instability. The complex political landscape of Pakistan, marked by power struggles between civilian and military institutions, posed significant obstacles to her administration's efforts to implement reforms. In 1990, her government was dismissed by the then-President Ghulam Ishaq Khan, citing corruption and economic mismanagement. Despite these setbacks, Benazir remained a resilient and determined leader, continuing her struggle for democracy and justice.

Benazir Bhutto's second term as Prime Minister, from 1993 to 1996, was also marked by efforts to advance her vision for Pakistan. She continued to focus on economic development, social welfare, and women's rights. Her government implemented policies aimed at privatizing state-owned enterprises, promoting foreign investment, and improving infrastructure. Benazir's administration also prioritized healthcare and education, launching initiatives to expand access to these essential services.

One of the key achievements of Benazir's second term was the establishment of the Benazir Income Support Programme (BISP), a social safety net aimed at providing financial assistance to low-income families. The BISP was a reflection of her commitment to addressing poverty and social inequality, and it remains one of the largest social welfare programs in Pakistan to this day. Benazir's efforts to improve the lives of ordinary Pakistanis through social welfare programs were central to her vision of a more just and equitable society.

Benazir Bhutto's leadership was characterized by her ability to inspire hope and resilience in the face of adversity. Despite the numerous challenges and obstacles she faced, including political opposition, military interference, and personal tragedy, she remained steadfast in her commitment to her principles and her vision for Pakistan. Her resilience and determination earned her admiration and support from millions of Pakistanis who saw her as a beacon of hope and a champion of democratic values.

Tragically, Benazir Bhutto's life and political career were cut short by her assassination on December 27, 2007. She was killed in a suicide attack while campaigning for the 2008 general elections. Her death was a profound loss for Pakistan and for the global community. Benazir's assassination underscored the deep-rooted challenges and dangers faced by those who advocate for democratic change in volatile political environments. Her martyrdom further solidified her legacy as a symbol of courage and resilience in the fight for democracy and social justice.

Benazir Bhutto's vision for Pakistan continues to inspire and influence political discourse in the country. Her legacy is carried forward by the Pakistan People's Party, which remains one of the major political forces in Pakistan. The PPP continues to advocate for the principles and values that Benazir championed, including democracy, social justice, and women's rights. Her children, Bilawal Bhutto Zardari and Asifa Bhutto Zardari, have also taken up her mantle, actively participating in politics and carrying forward her legacy.

Benazir's impact on women's empowerment in Pakistan is particularly noteworthy. As the first female Prime Minister of a Muslim-majority country, she broke significant barriers and paved the way for greater participation of women in politics and public life. Her leadership demonstrated that women could lead and govern effectively, challenging traditional gender norms and inspiring countless women and girls to pursue their aspirations. Benazir's advocacy for women's rights and gender equality remains a cornerstone of her legacy.

In addition to her contributions to Pakistani politics, Benazir Bhutto's legacy has had a global impact. She is remembered as a trailblazer for women in leadership and a vocal advocate for democracy and human rights. Her life and work have inspired numerous individuals and movements around the world, highlighting the importance of resilience, courage, and unwavering commitment to justice and equality.

Benazir Bhutto's vision for Pakistan was one of a democratic, progressive, and inclusive nation. Her leadership was marked by her dedication to addressing social inequalities, empowering marginalized communities, and promoting democratic values. Despite the numerous challenges and setbacks she faced, Benazir remained committed to her principles and her vision for a better Pakistan. Her legacy continues to inspire and guide those who strive for democratic governance, social justice, and human rights in Pakistan and beyond.

In conclusion, Benazir Bhutto's life and political career were characterized by her unwavering commitment to her vision for Pakistan. Her leadership, marked by resilience, determination, and a deep sense of justice, left an indelible mark on the nation's history. Benazir's efforts to promote democracy, social justice, and women's empowerment continue to inspire and influence political discourse in Pakistan and around the world. Her legacy serves as a powerful reminder of the importance of perseverance and courage in the pursuit of a more just and equitable society. Benazir Bhutto's vision for Pakistan remains a guiding light for those who continue to fight for democracy and social progress.

"Like a river carving its path through the rugged terrain, resilience flows through the landscape of our lives, shaping our journey with its unwavering strength and persistence."

THIRTEEN

WANGARI MAATHAI: THE GREEN BELT MOVEMENT

Wangari Maathai's name is indelibly linked with environmental activism, social justice, and the empowerment of women through her founding of the Green Belt Movement. Born on April 1, 1940, in Nyeri, Kenya, Maathai's early life was steeped in the traditions and natural beauty of the central highlands. Her deep connection to the land and a profound understanding of its importance to her community laid the foundation for her life's work in environmental conservation and sustainable development. Maathai's journey from a rural upbringing to becoming a globally recognized environmentalist and Nobel Peace Prize laureate is a story of relentless dedication, courage, and vision.

Maathai's academic journey began at a local primary school and continued through high school, where she excelled in her studies. Her academic prowess earned her a scholarship to study in the United States as part of the Kennedy Airlift program, an initiative that brought promising African students to American universities. Maathai attended Mount St. Scholastica College in Kansas, where she earned a degree in biological sciences. She then pursued a master's degree in biology at the University of Pittsburgh. These formative years in the United States exposed Maathai to the burgeoning environmental movement and the principles of ecological preservation, which would later influence her activism.

Upon returning to Kenya in 1966, Maathai embarked on an academic career, becoming the first woman in East and Central Africa to earn a doctorate. She joined the University of Nairobi as a veterinary anatomy professor, where she became involved in various civic and environmental organizations. During this period, Maathai began to recognize the critical links between environmental degradation, poverty, and women's rights. She observed that deforestation and unsustainable agricultural practices were leading to soil erosion, water scarcity, and declining agricultural productivity, which disproportionately affected rural women who relied on the land for their livelihoods.

In 1977, Wangari Maathai founded the Green Belt Movement, an environmental organization dedicated to combating deforestation, restoring ecosystems, and empowering women. The movement's core strategy was simple yet profound: planting trees to restore the environment and improve the quality of life for communities. The act of planting trees served multiple purposes: it provided a source of fuel, food, and income for rural communities, mitigated the effects of climate change, and conserved biodiversity. Moreover, it was a means of mobilizing and empowering women, who became the primary agents of change in their communities.

The Green Belt Movement's approach was deeply rooted in community participation and grassroots activism. Maathai understood that sustainable environmental conservation could only be achieved through the active involvement of local communities. The movement encouraged women to take the lead in planting and nurturing trees, providing them with training and resources to establish tree nurseries and manage reforestation projects. This approach not only promoted environmental sustainability but also fostered a sense of ownership and responsibility among the participants.

Maathai's work with the Green Belt Movement extended beyond tree planting. She championed broader issues of social justice, human rights, and democratic governance. Maathai recognized that environmental degradation was both a cause and a consequence of social and political inequities. She used the Green Belt Movement as a platform to advocate for greater transparency, accountability, and participation in decision-making processes. Her activism often brought her into direct conflict with the Kenyan government, which viewed her efforts as a threat to its authority.

One of the most notable examples of Maathai's defiance against government oppression occurred in the late 1980s and early 1990s when she led the campaign to prevent the construction of a massive skyscraper complex in Nairobi's Uhuru Park. The project, proposed by the government, would have resulted in significant environmental damage and the loss of public green space. Maathai's vocal opposition and grassroots mobilization garnered international attention and widespread public support. Despite facing intimidation, arrests, and physical violence, she successfully halted the project, preserving Uhuru Park for future generations.

Maathai's activism was not limited to environmental issues; she was a fierce advocate for women's rights and social justice. She believed that empowering women was essential for achieving sustainable development and social progress. The Green Belt Movement provided a platform for women to gain skills, confidence, and economic independence. Through tree planting and environmental conservation activities, women were able to generate income, improve their living conditions, and enhance their social status. Maathai's work highlighted the interconnectedness of environmental, social, and economic issues, emphasizing the need for holistic and inclusive approaches to development.

In recognition of her outstanding contributions to environmental conservation, democracy, and human rights, Wangari Maathai was awarded the Nobel Peace Prize in 2004. She became the first African woman to receive this prestigious honor. The Nobel Committee acknowledged her holistic approach to sustainable development, which integrated environmental protection with social and political empowerment. Maathai's receipt of the Nobel Peace Prize elevated the global visibility of the Green Belt Movement and inspired countless individuals and organizations to pursue similar initiatives.

Maathai's influence extended far beyond Kenya's borders. She became a prominent voice in the global environmental movement, participating in international conferences, advising governments, and collaborating with other environmental and human rights organizations. Her work emphasized the importance of grassroots activism and community-led solutions in addressing global challenges. Maathai's legacy is reflected in the numerous environmental and social initiatives that have been inspired by her vision and principles.

Throughout her life, Wangari Maathai faced numerous challenges and adversities. She endured political persecution, personal hardships, and societal resistance to her ideas and leadership. Despite these obstacles, she remained steadfast in her commitment to her vision and principles. Maathai's resilience, courage, and unwavering dedication to her cause continue to inspire activists and leaders around the world.

Wangari Maathai's legacy is not only about the millions of trees planted through the Green Belt Movement but also about the transformative impact of her work on communities and individuals. Her emphasis on empowerment, education, and community participation has left a lasting imprint on the environmental and social landscape. Maathai's approach to development, which integrates environmental sustainability with social justice and economic empowerment, offers valuable lessons for addressing contemporary global challenges.

The Green Belt Movement continues to thrive, carrying forward Maathai's vision and expanding its initiatives to address emerging environmental and social issues. The movement's programs now include climate change adaptation, renewable energy promotion, and advocacy for policy reforms. The organization's ongoing efforts reflect Maathai's belief in the power of collective action and the importance of nurturing a harmonious relationship between people and the environment.

Wangari Maathai's story is a powerful testament to the impact that one individual can have in effecting positive change. Her life and work exemplify the principles of courage, resilience, and visionary leadership. Maathai's contributions to environmental conservation, social justice, and women's empowerment have left an enduring legacy that continues to inspire and guide efforts towards a more sustainable and equitable world.

In conclusion, Wangari Maathai's founding of the Green Belt Movement was a groundbreaking initiative that addressed the interlinked challenges of environmental degradation, social inequality, and women's empowerment. Her holistic and inclusive approach to development has had a profound and lasting impact, both in Kenya and globally. Maathai's legacy as a visionary leader and tireless advocate for the environment and human rights serves as an enduring inspiration for all those committed to creating a better and more sustainable future. Her life's work reminds us of the power of grassroots activism, community participation, and the unwavering pursuit of justice and sustainability.

❧❧❧

"In the silence of solitude, find the echoes of your own resilience, for within the depths of your being lies the unwavering strength to weather any storm."

FOURTEEN

EMMA WATSON: HEFORSHE CAMPAIGN

Emma Watson, known globally for her role as Hermione Granger in the Harry Potter film series, has used her platform and influence to champion gender equality through the HeForShe campaign. Launched by UN Women in September 2014, HeForShe is a solidarity movement that calls on men and boys to become advocates for gender equality, challenging traditional gender norms and working alongside women to create a more just and equitable world. Emma Watson's involvement in this campaign has been pivotal, transforming her public persona from an actress to a globally recognized activist and advocate for women's rights.

Emma Watson's passion for gender equality was evident from an early age. Born on April 15, 1990, in Paris, France, and raised in England, she was acutely aware of gender disparities and the societal expectations placed on women. Her education at Brown University, where she studied English literature, further deepened her understanding of feminist theory and the importance of advocating for women's rights. Watson's global fame, coupled with her academic background and personal commitment to social justice, positioned her uniquely to make a significant impact in the fight for gender equality.

In her role as a UN Women Goodwill Ambassador, Emma Watson delivered a powerful and widely acclaimed speech at the United Nations Headquarters in New York to launch the HeForShe campaign. Her speech marked a defining moment in her activism, as she called for a global movement where men and boys would join women in the struggle for gender equality. Watson highlighted the restrictive nature of traditional gender roles, which harm both women and men. She emphasized that gender equality is not only a women's issue but a human rights issue that affects everyone.

Watson's speech was notable for its inclusive and persuasive rhetoric. She spoke about her own experiences with gender inequality, sharing personal anecdotes that resonated with a broad audience. She recounted how, at the age of eight, she was called "bossy" for wanting to direct a play, while boys were not. She discussed the social pressure she felt as a teenager to conform to feminine stereotypes and the confusion she experienced when her male friends could not express their emotions. By sharing these experiences, Watson underscored the pervasive nature of gender inequality and its impact on all aspects of life.

One of the key messages of the HeForShe campaign is that gender equality requires the active participation and support of men. Watson challenged the notion that feminism is synonymous with man-hating, clarifying that feminism is about equal rights and opportunities for all genders. She invited men to step forward as allies in the fight for gender equality, urging them to reflect on how societal expectations around masculinity limit their own freedoms and contribute to a culture of inequality. Watson's call to action was clear: men and boys must be part of the solution, working alongside women to dismantle systemic gender barriers.

The HeForShe campaign set ambitious goals to engage men and boys in the fight for gender equality. It encouraged individuals to take a public pledge to support gender equality and promoted the idea that small actions can lead to significant cultural shifts. The campaign aimed to create a global movement by leveraging the influence of high-profile individuals, corporations, universities, and governments. By engaging these stakeholders, HeForShe sought to drive systemic change and create environments where gender equality could flourish.

Emma Watson's advocacy through the HeForShe campaign has had a profound impact on raising awareness about gender equality issues. Her speech and ongoing efforts have sparked conversations around the world, challenging traditional gender norms and inspiring individuals to take action. The campaign has garnered support from millions of people, including high-profile figures such as Barack Obama, Ban Ki-moon, and Justin Trudeau, who have publicly pledged their support for gender equality. This widespread endorsement has helped to legitimize the campaign's goals and amplify its message.

Watson's influence extends beyond her public speeches and campaign appearances. She has used her social media platforms to engage with a global audience, sharing resources, stories, and updates related to gender equality. Her online presence has created a space for dialogue and education, where individuals can learn about feminist issues and connect with a broader community of advocates. By leveraging her celebrity status and digital reach, Watson has been able to mobilize a diverse and international audience, bridging the gap between celebrity activism and grassroots movements.

One of the significant achievements of the HeForShe campaign has been its ability to bring gender equality issues to the forefront of public discourse. By framing gender equality as a collective responsibility, the campaign has challenged traditional notions of feminism and created a more inclusive movement. The emphasis on solidarity and collaboration between genders has resonated with many, fostering a sense of shared purpose and commitment to social change. This approach has helped to break down the barriers that often prevent men from engaging in gender equality advocacy, encouraging them to become active participants in the movement.

The HeForShe campaign has also focused on addressing gender inequality within institutions, recognizing that systemic change is necessary to achieve lasting progress. The campaign's IMPACT 10x10x10 initiative, launched in 2015, targeted leaders in government, business, and academia to implement concrete commitments to gender equality. This initiative aimed to create a ripple effect, where institutional changes would lead to broader cultural shifts. By holding these institutions accountable and showcasing their progress, HeForShe has demonstrated that meaningful change is possible when there is a commitment to gender equality at the highest levels.

Emma Watson's involvement in the HeForShe campaign has also highlighted the importance of intersectionality in the fight for gender equality. She has acknowledged that gender inequality intersects with other forms of discrimination, including race, class, and sexual orientation. Watson's advocacy has emphasized the need for an inclusive feminism that addresses the diverse experiences and challenges faced by different groups of women. By promoting an intersectional approach, HeForShe aims to create a more comprehensive and equitable movement that leaves no one behind.

In addition to her work with HeForShe, Watson has continued to champion gender equality through various initiatives and projects. She has been a vocal supporter of the Time's Up movement, which addresses sexual harassment and assault in the workplace. Watson has also funded and supported organizations that provide legal aid to survivors of sexual violence. Her advocacy work extends to promoting education for girls, particularly in underserved communities, recognizing that access to education is a fundamental human right and a critical component of gender equality.

Emma Watson's journey as an activist has not been without challenges. She has faced criticism and backlash from those who oppose her views or question her motivations. However, Watson has remained steadfast in her commitment to gender equality, using her platform to advocate for change and amplify the voices of marginalized groups. Her resilience and determination have inspired many to join the fight for gender equality, demonstrating that even in the face of adversity, it is possible to make a difference.

The impact of the HeForShe campaign and Emma Watson's advocacy is evident in the growing global awareness and commitment to gender equality. The campaign has mobilized millions of individuals, encouraging them to take action in their communities and beyond. By fostering a sense of solidarity and shared responsibility, HeForShe has created a powerful movement that continues to challenge and transform societal norms. Watson's leadership has been instrumental in this process, proving that celebrity influence can be harnessed for meaningful social change.

In conclusion, Emma Watson's involvement in the HeForShe campaign represents a significant and impactful contribution to the global fight for gender equality. Her passionate advocacy, combined with her ability to engage and inspire a diverse audience, has helped to raise awareness about the importance of gender equality and the need for collective action. The HeForShe campaign's emphasis on solidarity, intersectionality, and institutional change has created a more inclusive and effective movement, challenging traditional gender norms and promoting a more just and equitable world. Watson's work continues to inspire and mobilize individuals around the globe, demonstrating the power of activism and the potential for lasting social change.

❦❦❦

"As the seasons change and the tides ebb and flow, so too does the landscape of our lives shift, yet through it all, resilience remains as the bedrock of our existence."

FIFTEEN

RUTH BADER GINSBURG: JUSTICE AND EQUALITY

Ruth Bader Ginsburg, widely known as RBG, was a pioneering advocate for justice and equality, whose work as a lawyer, professor, and Supreme Court Justice left an indelible mark on American law and society. Born on March 15, 1933, in Brooklyn, New York, Ginsburg grew up in a modest household where education and hard work were deeply valued. Her early life was marked by personal challenges, including the loss of her sister and mother, which instilled in her a resilience and determination that would define her career. Ginsburg's unwavering commitment to justice and equality, particularly in the realm of gender discrimination, transformed the legal landscape in the United States and inspired countless individuals around the world.

Ginsburg's academic journey was marked by excellence and perseverance. She graduated first in her class from Cornell University in 1954, where she met her future husband, Martin Ginsburg. The couple's partnership was one of mutual respect and support, crucial to both their professional and personal lives.

Ginsburg's pursuit of a legal career began at Harvard Law School, where she was one of only nine women in a class of over 500. Despite facing significant gender discrimination, Ginsburg excelled academically and later transferred to Columbia Law School, where she graduated first in her class in 1959. Her early career was marked by difficulty in securing employment due to her gender, but she eventually found a position as a clerk for Judge Edmund Palmieri of the U.S. District Court for the Southern District of New York.

Ginsburg's experiences with gender discrimination fueled her commitment to fighting for equality under the law. In the early 1960s, she began her academic career as a professor at Rutgers Law School, where she encountered further gender-based pay disparities. This experience galvanized her advocacy for women's rights, leading her to co-found the Women's Rights Law Reporter, the first law journal in the United States to focus exclusively on women's rights. Ginsburg's scholarly work laid the foundation for her future legal battles against gender discrimination.

In 1972, Ginsburg co-founded the Women's Rights Project at the American Civil Liberties Union (ACLU). As the project's director, she strategically litigated cases that challenged gender discrimination, carefully selecting cases that would set precedents and build a body of law that recognized gender equality as a fundamental right. Ginsburg's approach was methodical and incremental, aiming to demonstrate that gender discrimination harmed both women and men and was incompatible with the principles of equal protection enshrined in the Constitution.

One of Ginsburg's landmark cases was Reed v. Reed (1971), in which the Supreme Court struck down a law that automatically preferred men over women as estate administrators. This was the first time the Court applied the Equal Protection Clause of the Fourteenth Amendment to a case of gender discrimination. Ginsburg's argument, which highlighted the irrationality and unfairness of the law, set a significant precedent for future gender discrimination cases. Her success in Reed v. Reed paved the way for subsequent victories in cases such as Frontiero v. Richardson (1973), where the Court ruled that benefits given by the U.S. military could not be granted differently based on gender, and Weinberger v. Wiesenfeld (1975), which challenged the denial of Social Security benefits to widowers that were available to widows.

Ginsburg's work with the ACLU was instrumental in shifting the legal landscape towards greater gender equality. She argued six gender discrimination cases before the Supreme Court, winning five. Her arguments were characterized by their precision, logical coherence, and emphasis on the broader implications of gender-based laws. Ginsburg's strategic litigation and advocacy played a crucial role in dismantling many of the legal barriers that perpetuated gender discrimination, transforming the lives of countless individuals and advancing the cause of equality.

In 1980, President Jimmy Carter appointed Ginsburg to the U.S. Court of Appeals for the District of Columbia Circuit, where she served for thirteen years. Her tenure on the D.C. Circuit was marked by her careful, moderate jurisprudence and her ability to build consensus among her colleagues. Ginsburg's judicial philosophy was rooted in a deep respect for precedent and a belief in the incremental progress of the law. She was known for her meticulous attention to detail, her clear and concise writing, and her commitment to fairness and justice.

Ginsburg's elevation to the U.S. Supreme Court came in 1993 when President Bill Clinton nominated her to replace Justice Byron White. She was confirmed by the Senate in a 96-3 vote, reflecting broad bipartisan support for her appointment. As the second woman to serve on the Supreme Court, Ginsburg brought a unique perspective to the bench, informed by her extensive experience as a litigator and advocate for gender equality. Her tenure on the Supreme Court was marked by her unwavering commitment to justice, equality, and the protection of individual rights.

Ginsburg's judicial philosophy on the Supreme Court was characterized by her commitment to equality and her belief in the importance of a living Constitution that adapts to changing societal values. She was known for her powerful dissents, which often articulated a vision of justice and equality that challenged the majority's opinions. One of her most notable dissents was in the case of Ledbetter v. Goodyear Tire & Rubber Co. (2007), where the Court ruled against Lilly Ledbetter's pay discrimination claim. Ginsburg's dissent highlighted the ongoing issue of pay inequality and called on Congress to address the problem through legislation. Her dissent ultimately led to the passage of the Lilly Ledbetter Fair Pay Act in 2009, which restored workers' rights to challenge pay discrimination.

Another significant aspect of Ginsburg's jurisprudence was her advocacy for reproductive rights and gender equality in healthcare. In cases such as Gonzales v. Carhart (2007) and Burwell v. Hobby Lobby Stores, Inc. (2014), Ginsburg argued passionately for the protection of women's reproductive autonomy and the right to access healthcare without gender-based discrimination. Her opinions in these cases underscored her belief that gender equality and reproductive rights were fundamental to individual liberty and the pursuit of equality.

Ginsburg's impact extended beyond her judicial opinions to her role as a cultural and feminist icon. Her life and work inspired the "Notorious RBG" phenomenon, which celebrated her as a trailblazer and a symbol of resilience and justice. Ginsburg embraced her role as a cultural icon, using her platform to educate and inspire future generations. She was known for her rigorous workout routine, her distinctive style, and her ability to connect with people from all walks of life. Ginsburg's public appearances and speeches often emphasized the importance of civic engagement, the rule of law, and the ongoing struggle for justice and equality.

Throughout her life, Ginsburg faced personal and professional challenges with grace and determination. Her battle with cancer, which she faced multiple times, showcased her resilience and unwavering commitment to her work. Ginsburg's dedication to her role as a Supreme Court Justice, even in the face of serious illness, underscored her deep sense of duty and her belief in the importance of the judiciary in protecting individual rights and promoting justice.

Ginsburg's legacy is profound and multifaceted. Her work as a litigator, professor, and judge transformed the legal landscape and advanced the cause of gender equality in ways that continue to resonate today. She played a pivotal role in establishing legal protections against gender discrimination and advocating for the rights of women and marginalized communities. Ginsburg's judicial philosophy, characterized by her commitment to fairness, justice, and the protection of individual rights, has left an enduring impact on American law and society.

In her personal life, Ginsburg was known for her close and supportive relationship with her husband, Martin Ginsburg, a prominent tax attorney and law professor. Their partnership was one of mutual respect, love, and intellectual collaboration. Martin's unwavering support for Ginsburg's career and his role as an advocate for gender equality in his own right were instrumental in her success. Ginsburg often spoke of the importance of their partnership and the balance they struck between their professional and personal lives.

Ruth Bader Ginsburg's life and legacy continue to inspire and guide future generations. Her commitment to justice, equality, and the protection of individual rights serves as a powerful reminder of the importance of perseverance, resilience, and the ongoing struggle for a more just and equitable society. Ginsburg's work has left an indelible mark on the legal profession and has paved the way for future advocates and jurists to continue the fight for justice and equality.

In conclusion, Ruth Bader Ginsburg's legacy as a champion of justice and equality is unparalleled. Her pioneering work as a litigator and Supreme Court Justice transformed the legal landscape, advancing gender equality and protecting individual rights. Ginsburg's life and career are a testament to her resilience, determination, and unwavering commitment to justice. Her impact on American law and society will continue to be felt for generations to come, inspiring future generations to pursue the ideals of justice and equality that she so passionately championed.

"In the tapestry of humanity, resilience is the golden thread that binds us together, weaving a narrative of courage and triumph amidst the fabric of our shared experiences."

SIXTEEN

LEYMAH GBOWEE: PEACE AND RECONCILIATION

Leymah Gbowee is a remarkable figure whose dedication to peace and reconciliation has profoundly impacted Liberia and beyond. Born on February 1, 1972, in Monrovia, Liberia, Gbowee grew up during a time of relative stability in her country. However, her life took a dramatic turn when civil war broke out in Liberia in 1989, leading to years of violence, chaos, and suffering. Gbowee's journey from a young girl in war-torn Liberia to a Nobel Peace Prize laureate is a story of extraordinary courage, resilience, and unwavering commitment to peace.

The Liberian civil war, which lasted from 1989 to 2003, was characterized by brutal conflict, mass atrocities, and a devastating impact on the civilian population. The war claimed the lives of an estimated 250,000 people and displaced millions. Leymah Gbowee experienced firsthand the horrors of the conflict, which included witnessing widespread violence, losing loved ones, and enduring the hardships of displacement. These experiences left an indelible mark on her and fueled her determination to work for peace.

In the midst of the war, Gbowee found herself grappling with personal struggles, including an abusive relationship and the challenge of raising her children in a dangerous and unstable environment. Despite these hardships, she pursued an education in social work, which provided her with a deeper understanding of the social and psychological impacts of the conflict. This education, coupled with her personal experiences, equipped her with the knowledge and empathy needed to address the profound trauma experienced by her fellow Liberians.

Gbowee's path to becoming a peace activist began in earnest in 2002 when she joined the West Africa Network for Peacebuilding (WANEP). It was through WANEP that she became involved in the Women in Peacebuilding Network (WIPNET), an organization dedicated to mobilizing women to advocate for peace. Gbowee quickly emerged as a leader within WIPNET, recognizing the untapped potential of women to drive social and political change. She believed that women, who had borne the brunt of the war's violence and suffering, had a unique and powerful role to play in the peace process.

In 2003, Leymah Gbowee led the Women of Liberia Mass Action for Peace, a grassroots movement that brought together Christian and Muslim women in a unified call for an end to the war. This movement was unprecedented in its scope and impact. The women, dressed in white to symbolize peace, staged daily sit-ins and vigils, demanding that the warring factions negotiate a ceasefire and work towards a peace agreement. Their nonviolent protests garnered significant attention and support, both domestically and internationally.

One of the most dramatic and impactful actions taken by the Women of Liberia Mass Action for Peace was their protest at the peace talks held in Accra, Ghana, in 2003. Frustrated by the slow progress and intransigence of the negotiators, Gbowee and her fellow activists staged a sit-in, effectively barricading the meeting room and refusing to allow the negotiators to leave until they reached a resolution. This bold and courageous act of civil disobedience put immense pressure on the parties involved and contributed to the eventual signing of the Accra Comprehensive Peace Agreement, which marked the end of the civil war.

The success of the Women of Liberia Mass Action for Peace was a testament to the power of grassroots activism and the critical role of women in peacebuilding. Gbowee's leadership and vision were instrumental in uniting women across religious and ethnic divides, demonstrating that solidarity and nonviolent resistance could bring about meaningful change. The movement also highlighted the importance of inclusivity in peace processes, ensuring that the voices and perspectives of those most affected by the conflict were heard and considered.

Following the end of the civil war, Gbowee continued her work in peacebuilding and reconciliation. She founded the Women Peace and Security Network Africa (WIPSEN-Africa), an organization dedicated to promoting women's participation in peace and security efforts across the continent. Through WIPSEN-Africa, Gbowee has worked to empower women, build their capacity as leaders, and advocate for their inclusion in decision-making processes at all levels. Her efforts have had a lasting impact, contributing to greater gender equality and the recognition of women's vital contributions to peace and security.

In recognition of her extraordinary work, Leymah Gbowee was awarded the Nobel Peace Prize in 2011, along with Ellen Johnson Sirleaf and Tawakkol Karman. The Nobel Committee praised Gbowee for her "nonviolent struggle for the safety of women and for women's rights to full participation in peacebuilding work." The award brought international attention to her efforts and underscored the critical role of women in promoting peace and reconciliation.

Gbowee's influence extends beyond Liberia and Africa. She has become a global advocate for peace, women's rights, and social justice, sharing her experiences and insights with audiences around the world. Her autobiography, "Mighty Be Our Powers: How Sisterhood, Prayer, and Sex Changed a Nation at War," provides a powerful account of her journey and the transformative impact of the women's peace movement in Liberia. Gbowee's story has inspired countless individuals and organizations to embrace the principles of nonviolence, solidarity, and grassroots activism in their own efforts to address conflict and promote social change.

One of the central themes of Gbowee's work is the importance of addressing the root causes of conflict and creating sustainable peace. She has consistently emphasized the need for comprehensive approaches that address the social, economic, and political factors that contribute to violence. Gbowee's advocacy for education, economic empowerment, and social inclusion reflects her understanding that peace is not simply the absence of conflict but the presence of justice, equality, and opportunity for all.

Gbowee's commitment to reconciliation is also evident in her efforts to heal the wounds of war and foster national unity. She has worked to support trauma healing and reconciliation programs, recognizing the deep psychological scars left by the conflict. Her emphasis on forgiveness, dialogue, and restorative justice has helped to build bridges between communities and promote a sense of shared humanity. Gbowee's approach to reconciliation is grounded in her belief in the power of empathy, compassion, and the transformative potential of individuals and communities to overcome division and hatred.

Throughout her career, Gbowee has faced numerous challenges and obstacles, including political resistance, cultural barriers, and personal sacrifices. Despite these difficulties, she has remained steadfast in her commitment to her principles and her vision for a more just and peaceful world. Her resilience and determination have been a source of inspiration for many, demonstrating that meaningful change is possible even in the face of seemingly insurmountable odds.

Leymah Gbowee's legacy is a testament to the power of ordinary individuals to effect extraordinary change. Her leadership in the Women of Liberia Mass Action for Peace and her ongoing efforts in peacebuilding and reconciliation have had a profound impact on her country and the world. Gbowee's work serves as a powerful reminder of the importance of women's participation in peace processes and the critical role of grassroots activism in driving social and political change.

In conclusion, Leymah Gbowee's dedication to peace and reconciliation has left an enduring legacy that continues to inspire and guide efforts towards a more just and equitable world. Her leadership, vision, and unwavering commitment to nonviolence and social justice have transformed the lives of countless individuals and communities. Gbowee's work underscores the importance of addressing the root causes of conflict, empowering marginalized groups, and fostering a culture of empathy and compassion. Her story is a powerful example of the potential for individuals and communities to create lasting and meaningful change through solidarity, resilience, and the pursuit of justice.

❦❦❦

"Like a phoenix emerging from the ashes, let
resilience be the flame that ignites your spirit,
casting a radiant glow upon the darkest corners of
despair."

SEVENTEEN

HILLARY CLINTON: WOMEN'S RIGHTS ARE HUMAN RIGHTS

Hillary Clinton's declaration that "women's rights are human rights" during her landmark speech at the United Nations Fourth World Conference on Women in Beijing in 1995 was a pivotal moment in the global fight for gender equality. This assertion, delivered with clarity and conviction, resonated across the globe and cemented her legacy as a champion for women's rights. Throughout her career, Hillary Clinton has been a relentless advocate for gender equality, using her platform as First Lady, U.S. Senator, Secretary of State, and presidential candidate to advance the cause of women's rights and social justice.

Born on October 26, 1947, in Chicago, Illinois, Hillary Diane Rodham Clinton grew up in a middle-class family where her parents emphasized the importance of education and hard work. She excelled academically, attending Wellesley College and later Yale Law School, where she met her future husband, Bill Clinton. Her early career included working as a lawyer and a child advocate, which laid the foundation for her lifelong commitment to public service and social justice.

Clinton's tenure as First Lady of Arkansas and later as First Lady of the United States provided her with a unique platform to advocate for various social issues, including children's rights, healthcare reform, and gender equality. Her involvement in these issues demonstrated her deep commitment to improving the lives of women and families. However, it was her speech at the Beijing Conference that marked a significant turning point in her advocacy for women's rights on the global stage.

The Beijing Conference, held in September 1995, brought together delegates from around the world to discuss and address issues related to gender equality and women's empowerment. At this historic gathering, Clinton delivered a powerful speech that unequivocally linked women's rights to human rights. She stated, "If there is one message that echoes forth from this conference, it is that human rights are women's rights and women's rights are human rights, once and for all." This declaration was a bold and unequivocal affirmation of the fundamental importance of gender equality in the broader human rights agenda.

Clinton's speech highlighted the pervasive discrimination and violence faced by women worldwide. She spoke out against practices such as domestic violence, forced marriage, female genital mutilation, and the denial of education and healthcare to women and girls. By addressing these issues head-on, Clinton brought global attention to the systemic injustices that women face and called for concerted international efforts to combat them. Her speech was a call to action, urging governments, organizations, and individuals to recognize and address the human rights abuses suffered by women.

One of the key messages of Clinton's speech was the interconnectedness of women's rights and broader social and economic development. She argued that empowering women and ensuring their rights are protected is not only a moral imperative but also essential for the progress and prosperity of societies. Clinton emphasized that when women are educated, healthy, and free from violence and discrimination, they can contribute more effectively to their families, communities, and nations. This holistic approach to gender equality underscored the importance of integrating women's rights into all aspects of development policy and practice.

Following the Beijing Conference, Clinton continued to advocate for women's rights through various initiatives and policy efforts. As First Lady, she played a key role in the creation of the Office on Violence Against Women within the U.S. Department of Justice, which aimed to improve the response to domestic violence and support survivors. Her efforts contributed to the passage of the Violence Against Women Act in 1994, a landmark piece of legislation that provided critical resources and support for victims of domestic violence and sexual assault.

Clinton's advocacy for women's rights extended beyond her tenure as First Lady. As a U.S. Senator from New York, she championed legislation aimed at promoting gender equality and supporting women's health and economic empowerment. She introduced and supported bills addressing issues such as pay equity, family leave, and reproductive rights. Her legislative efforts were guided by her belief in the importance of creating a more equitable society where women have equal opportunities to succeed and thrive.

As Secretary of State under President Barack Obama, Clinton made women's rights a central focus of U.S. foreign policy. She established the Office of Global Women's Issues and appointed an Ambassador-at-Large for Global Women's Issues to coordinate efforts to promote gender equality worldwide. Clinton's tenure as Secretary of State was marked by her emphasis on the role of women in peace and security, recognizing that women's participation is essential for sustainable development and conflict resolution. She championed initiatives such as the National Action Plan on Women, Peace, and Security, which aimed to enhance the role of women in preventing and resolving conflicts.

Clinton's leadership in promoting women's rights on the global stage included advocating for women's economic empowerment. She highlighted the economic benefits of gender equality, emphasizing that empowering women economically leads to greater economic growth and stability. Clinton's initiatives focused on increasing women's access to education, financial services, and economic opportunities. She launched programs to support women entrepreneurs and improve women's access to markets and resources, recognizing that economic empowerment is a critical component of achieving gender equality.

ᐅᐅᐅ

One of the enduring impacts of Clinton's advocacy for women's rights is her role in changing the global discourse on gender equality. Her speeches, policy initiatives, and public statements have consistently highlighted the importance of addressing gender-based discrimination and violence. Clinton's ability to articulate the connections between women's rights and broader human rights issues has helped to elevate the conversation and inspire action at both the national and international levels.

Clinton's 2016 presidential campaign further underscored her commitment to gender equality. She became the first woman to be nominated for president by a major U.S. political party, breaking a significant barrier and inspiring women and girls around the world. Her campaign platform included comprehensive policies aimed at promoting women's rights, such as closing the gender pay gap, expanding family leave, and protecting reproductive rights.

Although she did not win the election, her candidacy represented a significant step forward in the fight for gender equality and women's political representation.

Throughout her career, Clinton has faced criticism and challenges, often rooted in the very gender biases she has sought to dismantle. She has been scrutinized for her policy decisions, personal life, and public statements in ways that are often disproportionate compared to her male counterparts. Despite these challenges, Clinton has remained steadfast in her commitment to advocating for women's rights and social justice. Her resilience and determination have been a source of inspiration for many, demonstrating that progress often requires perseverance and courage in the face of adversity.

Hillary Clinton's impact on women's rights and gender equality is profound and far-reaching. Her advocacy has contributed to significant policy changes, raised global awareness about the importance of gender equality, and inspired a new generation of activists and leaders. Clinton's declaration that "women's rights are human rights" continues to resonate as a powerful and enduring affirmation of the fundamental importance of gender equality. Her legacy as a champion for women's rights is a testament to her unwavering commitment to justice, equality, and the empowerment of women worldwide.

In conclusion, Hillary Clinton's career and advocacy for women's rights have had a transformative impact on the global fight for gender equality. Her declaration that "women's rights are human rights" at the Beijing Conference in 1995 marked a pivotal moment in the movement, bringing global attention to the systemic injustices faced by women and calling for concerted action to address them. Clinton's work as First Lady, U.S. Senator, Secretary of State, and presidential candidate has consistently advanced the cause of women's rights, promoting policies and initiatives aimed at achieving gender equality and empowering women. Her legacy as a champion for women's rights continues to inspire and guide efforts towards a more just and equitable world, highlighting the importance of perseverance, courage, and the ongoing struggle for gender equality.

"In the crucible of adversity, resilience is forged as
the steel of our souls, tempered by the fires of
challenge and adversity, emerging stronger and
more resilient than before."

EIGHTEEN

ELLEN JOHNSON SIRLEAF: LEADING LIBERIA

Ellen Johnson Sirleaf's leadership of Liberia marked a transformative period in the country's history, bringing stability, economic recovery, and a commitment to democratic governance after years of civil war and turmoil. Born on October 29, 1938, in Monrovia, Liberia, Johnson Sirleaf grew up in a society where political participation for women was limited, yet she rose to become Africa's first elected female head of state. Her journey to the presidency was marked by resilience, education, and a profound dedication to public service, which she utilized to lead Liberia through some of its most challenging times.

Johnson Sirleaf's early life was influenced by her family's values and her drive for education. She attended the College of West Africa in Monrovia and later earned a degree in accounting from Madison Business College in Wisconsin, USA. She furthered her studies at the University of Colorado and obtained a Master of Public Administration degree from Harvard University's John F. Kennedy School of Government. These academic achievements equipped her with the knowledge and skills necessary for a career in public service and economic management.

Her early career included positions in the Liberian government, where she served as Assistant Minister of Finance under President William Tolbert. However, her tenure was cut short by a military coup in 1980 led by Samuel Doe, which plunged Liberia into political instability. Johnson Sirleaf fled into exile, where she worked for various international organizations, including the World Bank and Citibank, and served as Director of the United Nations Development Programme's Regional Bureau for Africa. These roles provided her with a global perspective on development and governance, further shaping her vision for Liberia's future.

The Liberian civil wars, spanning from 1989 to 2003, were a period of devastating conflict that resulted in the loss of approximately 250,000 lives and displaced countless others. The country's infrastructure was decimated, and the social fabric was torn apart. Throughout this period, Johnson Sirleaf remained a vocal critic of the warring factions and advocated for peace and reconciliation. Her political involvement during these turbulent times included running for president in the 1997 elections, where she lost to Charles Taylor amidst allegations of electoral fraud and intimidation.

Following Taylor's exile and the end of the civil war in 2003, Liberia faced the monumental task of reconstruction and reconciliation. In this context, Johnson Sirleaf emerged as a symbol of hope and stability. Her extensive experience in public administration and international development positioned her as a capable leader for the nation's recovery. In the 2005 presidential election, she campaigned on a platform of reform, transparency, and economic development, ultimately winning and making history as the first elected female president in Africa.

Johnson Sirleaf's presidency was characterized by efforts to stabilize and rebuild Liberia. One of her administration's primary goals was to restore basic services and infrastructure, including healthcare, education, and transportation. Under her leadership, Liberia saw improvements in these areas, with increased access to primary education, the construction and renovation of healthcare facilities, and the rehabilitation of major roads. These developments were crucial for improving the quality of life for Liberians and laying the foundation for sustainable growth.

Economic recovery was another cornerstone of Johnson Sirleaf's tenure. She focused on attracting foreign investment, rebuilding the nation's economy, and managing its debt. Her administration negotiated significant debt relief agreements, which helped to alleviate the burden of Liberia's external debt and create fiscal space for development initiatives. Johnson Sirleaf also prioritized reforms in the natural resource sector, aiming to ensure that revenues from Liberia's rich mineral and forestry resources were used transparently and benefited the broader population.

Corruption was a pervasive issue in Liberia, and Johnson Sirleaf's administration took steps to combat it. She established the Liberia Anti-Corruption Commission (LACC) and implemented various measures to promote transparency and accountability in government. While progress in curbing corruption was uneven and faced significant challenges, her efforts represented a commitment to building a more transparent and accountable governance system.

Johnson Sirleaf's leadership extended beyond economic and infrastructural development to addressing the social and psychological impacts of the civil wars. She prioritized national reconciliation, promoting dialogue and understanding among Liberia's diverse ethnic and political groups. The Truth and Reconciliation Commission (TRC) was established to investigate human rights abuses committed during the conflict and provide a platform for victims and perpetrators to share their experiences.

Although the TRC's recommendations were met with mixed reactions and implementation challenges, it was a step towards healing and national unity.

Education and women's empowerment were central to Johnson Sirleaf's vision for Liberia. She believed that educating girls and empowering women were essential for the country's development. Her administration supported initiatives to improve girls' access to education, reduce gender-based violence, and increase women's participation in politics and business.

Johnson Sirleaf's own rise to the presidency served as an inspiration to women and girls in Liberia and across Africa, demonstrating the importance of female leadership and participation in governance.

The Ebola epidemic of 2014-2016 posed one of the most significant challenges during Johnson Sirleaf's presidency. The outbreak, which claimed over 4,800 lives in Liberia, exposed weaknesses in the country's healthcare system and posed a severe threat to its social and economic stability. Johnson Sirleaf's government, in collaboration with international partners, implemented measures to contain the virus, including public health campaigns, the establishment of treatment centers, and the mobilization of healthcare workers.

Her leadership during the crisis was instrumental in eventually bringing the outbreak under control, although it left a lasting impact on Liberia's healthcare system and economy.

Johnson Sirleaf's presidency also focused on strengthening Liberia's democratic institutions. She worked to promote free and fair elections, judicial independence, and respect for human rights. Her commitment to democratic principles was evident in her decision to step down after two terms in office, in accordance with the constitution, despite calls for her to seek an extension. This decision set a precedent for democratic transitions in Liberia and underscored the importance of adhering to the rule of law.

Internationally, Johnson Sirleaf was a respected stateswoman and advocate for African development and women's leadership. She used her platform to highlight issues such as poverty, gender inequality, and the need for global cooperation in addressing development challenges.

Her contributions were recognized with numerous awards and honors, including the Nobel Peace Prize in 2011, which she shared with Leymah Gbowee and Tawakkol Karman for their nonviolent struggle for the safety of women and for women's rights to full participation in peacebuilding work.

Johnson Sirleaf's post-presidency period has continued to reflect her commitment to leadership and development. She remains active in various international organizations and initiatives, focusing on issues such as health, education, and women's empowerment. Her memoir, "This Child Will Be Great," offers an insightful account of her life and leadership journey, providing valuable lessons on resilience, courage, and the pursuit of justice.

Ellen Johnson Sirleaf's leadership of Liberia is a testament to the power of vision, determination, and integrity. Her tenure as president brought stability, hope, and progress to a nation scarred by decades of conflict.

Through her efforts to rebuild infrastructure, promote economic recovery, combat corruption, and foster national reconciliation, she laid the foundation for a more prosperous and democratic Liberia. Johnson Sirleaf's legacy as a trailblazer for women's leadership and a champion of human rights continues to inspire individuals and leaders worldwide, demonstrating the profound impact of dedicated and compassionate leadership.

❦❦❦

"As the moon waxes and wanes in the night sky, so too does the ebb and flow of life's challenges, yet within us burns the eternal flame of resilience, guiding us through the darkness."

NINETEEN

SHIRIN EBADI: ADVOCATING FOR HUMAN RIGHTS IN IRAN

Shirin Ebadi's tireless advocacy for human rights in Iran has made her a global symbol of courage and resilience. Born on June 21, 1947, in Hamadan, Iran, Ebadi grew up in a society deeply rooted in traditional values. Despite these constraints, she pursued a legal career and became one of the first female judges in Iran, marking the beginning of a lifelong commitment to justice and equality. Her journey from a prominent judge to a human rights activist reflects the broader struggle for human rights and democracy in Iran, a country with a complex political landscape marked by authoritarian rule and repression.

Ebadi's early life was shaped by her family's emphasis on education and justice. Her father, a professor of commercial law, influenced her decision to pursue a career in law. She attended the University of Tehran, where she earned a law degree and later a doctorate in private law. In 1969, she became one of the first women in Iran to serve as a judge, a significant achievement in a male-dominated profession. However, her judicial career was abruptly interrupted following the 1979 Iranian Revolution, which led to the establishment of an Islamic Republic. The new regime dismissed all female judges, relegating Ebadi to clerical duties.

The revolution profoundly altered Iran's political and social landscape, imposing strict religious and gender norms that significantly curtailed women's rights. Ebadi, stripped of her judicial position, refused to be silenced. She used this setback as a catalyst to advocate for legal and human rights reforms. She resumed practicing law privately and took on cases that others shied away from, defending political dissidents, journalists, and women facing discrimination. Her legal practice became a platform for challenging the injustices perpetuated by the regime.

Ebadi's work as a lawyer was marked by a series of high-profile cases that highlighted the systemic human rights abuses in Iran. She defended numerous clients who had been unjustly imprisoned or persecuted for their political beliefs or activism. One notable case was that of the family of Dariush and Parvaneh Forouhar, political activists who were brutally murdered by government agents. Ebadi's relentless pursuit of justice in this case brought international attention to the regime's use of violence and intimidation against its critics.

In addition to her legal practice, Ebadi was deeply involved in promoting children's and women's rights. She founded the Society for Protecting the Rights of the Child in 1995, focusing on issues such as child labor, juvenile justice, and children's access to education. Her work with the organization underscored the broader social and economic challenges facing Iran's younger generation. Ebadi also co-founded the Defenders of Human Rights Center, which provided legal assistance to those targeted by the regime and documented human rights abuses.

Ebadi's activism was not without significant personal risk. Her outspoken criticism of the government and her defense of marginalized groups made her a target for harassment, intimidation, and legal persecution. She faced numerous threats to her safety and was subjected to surveillance and raids by security forces. Despite these dangers, she remained undeterred, driven by a steadfast commitment to justice and human rights.

In 2003, Shirin Ebadi was awarded the Nobel Peace Prize, becoming the first Iranian and the first Muslim woman to receive the honor. The Nobel Committee recognized her "efforts for democracy and human rights," particularly her focus on the rights of women and children. The award brought international acclaim to Ebadi's work and drew global attention to the human rights situation in Iran. In her Nobel lecture, Ebadi emphasized the universality of human rights and the importance of upholding these principles regardless of cultural or religious context.

The Nobel Prize significantly elevated Ebadi's profile and provided her with a larger platform to advocate for human rights. She used her newfound visibility to amplify her calls for reform and to support other human rights defenders. Ebadi continued to speak out against the Iranian government's repressive policies and to advocate for greater political freedom and social justice. Her work inspired many within Iran and around the world, demonstrating the power of individual courage in the face of authoritarianism.

However, the Iranian government's response to Ebadi's international recognition was harsh. Authorities intensified their efforts to silence her, targeting her family and colleagues. In 2009, amidst a crackdown on political dissent following the disputed presidential election, Ebadi was forced into exile. Her office was raided, and her assets were seized. Despite being driven out of her home country, Ebadi continued her activism from abroad, undeterred by the regime's attempts to stifle her voice.

Living in exile, Ebadi has remained a vocal advocate for human rights in Iran. She has continued to work with international organizations, such as the United Nations, to highlight human rights abuses and to call for international solidarity with the Iranian people. Ebadi's advocacy extends to a broad range of issues, including freedom of expression, political imprisonment, and the rights of ethnic and religious minorities. Her writings, including books and articles, have provided a critical perspective on the situation in Iran and have contributed to the global discourse on human rights and democracy.

Ebadi's life and work exemplify the broader struggle for human rights in Iran, a country where activists and dissidents face severe repression. The Iranian regime's tactics of intimidation, imprisonment, and violence are designed to suppress any challenge to its authority. Despite these oppressive conditions, individuals like Ebadi continue to resist, demonstrating remarkable resilience and determination. Their efforts are crucial in keeping the hope for democratic change and human rights alive in Iran.

Ebadi's advocacy also highlights the interconnectedness of various social justice issues. She has consistently argued that women's rights, children's rights, and human rights are inseparable. Her work underscores the importance of a holistic approach to social justice, recognizing that discrimination and oppression in one area often reinforce and exacerbate inequalities in others. This intersectional perspective is vital for understanding and addressing the complex realities of human rights abuses in Iran and beyond.

The impact of Shirin Ebadi's work extends beyond Iran's borders. Her advocacy has inspired a global movement for human rights and has highlighted the importance of international solidarity in the face of repression. Ebadi's story is a powerful reminder of the potential for individuals to effect change, even in the most challenging circumstances. Her unwavering commitment to justice and equality serves as an inspiration to human rights defenders worldwide.

In conclusion, Shirin Ebadi's advocacy for human rights in Iran represents a courageous and relentless struggle against systemic oppression and injustice. Her journey from a prominent judge to a leading human rights activist reflects her deep commitment to justice, equality, and the rule of law. Despite facing significant personal risk and exile, Ebadi has remained steadfast in her efforts to promote human rights and to support those who are marginalized and persecuted. Her work has brought global attention to the human rights situation in Iran and has inspired countless individuals to continue the fight for justice and democracy. Ebadi's legacy is a testament to the power of resilience, courage, and the enduring pursuit of human rights.

ppp

"In the garden of life, resilience is the seed from
which courage blossoms, its roots anchored deep
within the soil of our souls, nourished by the waters
of perseverance."

TWENTY

THE FUTURE OF WOMEN'S VOICES

The future of women's voices is a subject of immense significance in the ongoing discourse on gender equality and social justice. Over the past century, the global movement for women's rights has made substantial progress, yet much remains to be done. As we look ahead, the amplification of women's voices will be crucial in addressing the complex and interconnected challenges of the 21st century. This future is shaped by the diverse experiences and perspectives of women worldwide, driven by their resilience, creativity, and determination to effect change. The next steps in this journey involve ensuring greater representation, addressing systemic inequalities, leveraging technology, and fostering inclusive environments where women's voices can thrive.

One of the most significant aspects of the future of women's voices is the push for greater representation in all spheres of society. Historically, women have been underrepresented in politics, business, academia, and other areas of public life. This lack of representation has led to policies and practices that often fail to address the unique needs and perspectives of women. Increasing the number of women in leadership positions is crucial for creating more inclusive and equitable systems. This involves not only encouraging women to pursue these roles but also dismantling the structural barriers that prevent them from doing so. Efforts to achieve gender parity in political offices, corporate boards, and educational institutions are essential steps toward ensuring that women's voices are heard and valued.

The intersectionality of gender with other social identities such as race, class, sexuality, and ability is another critical consideration for the future of women's voices. Women from marginalized communities often face compounded forms of discrimination, which can further silence their voices. Recognizing and addressing these intersecting oppressions is vital for creating a more inclusive feminist movement. It involves amplifying the voices of women who have been historically marginalized and ensuring that their experiences and perspectives are integral to the conversation on gender equality. This requires a commitment to intersectional feminism, which acknowledges the diverse and multifaceted nature of women's experiences and advocates for systemic change that benefits all women.

The role of technology in amplifying women's voices cannot be overstated. The digital age has provided unprecedented opportunities for women to connect, share their stories, and advocate for change. Social media platforms, online forums, and digital publications have become powerful tools for grassroots activism and global movements. Campaigns like #MeToo and #TimesUp have demonstrated the transformative potential of digital activism in raising awareness and holding perpetrators of gender-based violence accountable. These movements have empowered women to share their experiences, challenge societal norms, and demand justice. The continued evolution of digital platforms will play a crucial role in the future of women's voices, providing new avenues for advocacy, education, and community building.

However, the digital realm also presents challenges that must be addressed to ensure it remains a safe and inclusive space for women. Online harassment, cyberbullying, and the spread of misogynistic content can silence women's voices and discourage them from participating in digital spaces. Efforts to combat online abuse, promote digital literacy, and create supportive online communities are essential for empowering women to use technology effectively. This involves both policy interventions and cultural shifts that prioritize respect, inclusion, and accountability in digital interactions.

Education remains a fundamental pillar in the empowerment of women's voices. Access to quality education equips women with the knowledge, skills, and confidence needed to advocate for their rights and participate fully in society. While significant strides have been made in increasing girls' access to education, disparities persist, particularly in low-income and conflict-affected regions. Investing in education, particularly for girls and women, is critical for building a future where women's voices are strong and influential. This includes not only primary and secondary education but also opportunities for higher education and lifelong learning. Educational curricula that promote gender equality, critical thinking, and leadership skills can further empower women to become change-makers in their communities and beyond.

Economic empowerment is another key factor in amplifying women's voices. Financial independence allows women to make choices about their lives, advocate for their rights, and contribute to their communities. Addressing the gender pay gap, ensuring equal access to employment opportunities, and supporting women entrepreneurs are crucial steps toward economic empowerment. Policies that promote work-life balance, such as parental leave and affordable childcare, also play a vital role in enabling women to participate fully in the workforce. Economic empowerment initiatives should be designed to reach women in all sectors, including those in informal and marginalized economies, ensuring that all women have the opportunity to thrive.

The future of women's voices also depends on the continued efforts to address gender-based violence and discrimination. Despite global advancements in women's rights, gender-based violence remains pervasive, affecting millions of women worldwide. Efforts to combat this issue must include comprehensive legal frameworks, effective enforcement mechanisms, and support services for survivors. Public awareness campaigns, education programs, and community initiatives can also play a critical role in challenging cultural norms and attitudes that perpetuate violence and discrimination. Creating safe environments where women can speak out without fear of retribution is essential for empowering them to advocate for their rights and those of others.

Health and reproductive rights are fundamental to the empowerment of women's voices. Access to comprehensive healthcare, including reproductive health services, enables women to make informed decisions about their bodies and lives. Ensuring that women have access to safe and legal abortion, contraception, and maternal healthcare is critical for their autonomy and well-being. Health policies must be inclusive and responsive to the needs of all women, recognizing the diverse factors that influence health outcomes. Addressing health disparities and promoting gender-sensitive healthcare can significantly enhance women's ability to participate fully in society.

The arts and media play a powerful role in shaping cultural narratives and amplifying women's voices. Representation in film, literature, music, and other forms of media can challenge stereotypes, promote positive role models, and highlight women's contributions to society. Encouraging diverse and authentic portrayals of women in media can help to shift cultural perceptions and promote gender equality. Supporting women in creative industries, providing platforms for their work, and promoting media literacy are essential for ensuring that women's voices are heard and celebrated.

Policy advocacy and legal reforms are crucial components of the future of women's voices. Laws and policies that promote gender equality and protect women's rights are foundational to creating a just and equitable society. Advocacy efforts must continue to push for legislative changes that address gender discrimination, protect against violence, and promote equal opportunities. Engaging with policymakers, building coalitions, and mobilizing communities are essential strategies for driving policy change. Legal reforms should be accompanied by efforts to ensure their effective implementation and enforcement, ensuring that women can access justice and hold perpetrators accountable.

Global cooperation and solidarity are also vital for advancing the future of women's voices. The challenges faced by women are often interconnected and transcend national boundaries. International organizations, governments, and civil society must work together to promote gender equality and protect women's rights. Collaborative efforts, such as the United Nations' Sustainable Development Goals, provide a framework for addressing global gender disparities and promoting women's empowerment. Solidarity among women's movements worldwide can amplify their impact, share best practices, and build a united front against gender-based injustices.

The future of women's voices is inherently linked to the broader struggle for social justice and human rights. Women's rights are human rights, and the fight for gender equality is inseparable from the fight for a just and equitable world. As we look to the future, it is essential to recognize the interconnectedness of various social justice issues and work towards comprehensive and inclusive solutions. Women's voices must be at the forefront of this effort, driving change and advocating for a world where everyone, regardless of gender, can live with dignity, freedom, and equality.

In conclusion, the future of women's voices is a dynamic and evolving landscape that requires continued effort, innovation, and commitment. Ensuring greater representation, addressing systemic inequalities, leveraging technology, and fostering inclusive environments are critical steps toward amplifying women's voices. By embracing intersectionality, promoting education and economic empowerment, combating gender-based violence, and advocating for legal reforms, we can create a future where women's voices are powerful and influential. The journey toward gender equality is ongoing, and the voices of women will continue to be a driving force in shaping a more just and equitable world.

❦❦❦

"With each sunrise, we are granted the gift of
resilience, a beacon of hope that illuminates the
path forward, guiding us through the shadows
towards the light of a new day."

TWENTY-ONE
SUMMARY

The voices of women have long been instrumental in shaping the world's socio-political landscape, advocating for justice, equality, and the upliftment of marginalized communities. This collection of essays captures the essence of the contributions made by some of the most influential women in modern history, each of whom has left an indelible mark on society through their tireless advocacy and leadership. From political figures and environmental activists to champions of human rights and gender equality, these women have navigated diverse challenges to amplify their voices and effect meaningful change.

Michelle Obama's tenure as First Lady of the United States exemplified the power of compassionate leadership. Her initiatives, such as the "Let Girls Learn" and "Reach Higher" programs, underscored her commitment to education and empowerment. By promoting healthy lifestyles through the "Let's Move!" campaign and advocating for the rights and opportunities of women and girls globally, Michelle Obama demonstrated how a public figure could leverage their influence to create positive societal change. Her ability to connect personally with people, coupled with her emphasis on kindness and empathy, continues to inspire future generations.

Greta Thunberg's emergence as a leading voice for climate change brought a sense of urgency to environmental activism. Starting with a solo school strike, her movement grew into the global "Fridays for Future" initiative, rallying millions of young people worldwide to demand immediate action on climate change. Thunberg's clear, direct communication and reliance on scientific evidence have challenged world leaders to confront the climate crisis head-on. Her activism highlights the critical role of youth in advocating for sustainable futures and has underscored the importance of individual and collective action in addressing global environmental challenges.

Jacinda Ardern's leadership of New Zealand during times of crisis showcased the effectiveness of compassionate governance. Her empathetic response to the Christchurch mosque shootings and her decisive action during the COVID-19 pandemic demonstrated her ability to balance empathy with pragmatism. Ardern's focus on social justice, economic development, and environmental sustainability has set a benchmark for inclusive and progressive leadership. Her efforts to promote gender equality and address systemic inequalities have further cemented her legacy as a transformative leader in contemporary politics.

Benazir Bhutto's historic rise to become the first female Prime Minister of Pakistan broke significant barriers and set a precedent for women's political participation in Muslim-majority countries. Her tenure was marked by efforts to promote economic development, social justice, and women's rights amidst political instability and challenges. Bhutto's leadership emphasized the importance of education, healthcare, and social welfare in building a more equitable society. Despite facing political opposition and personal tragedy, her vision for a democratic and progressive Pakistan continues to inspire leaders and advocates worldwide.

Wangari Maathai's Green Belt Movement in Kenya demonstrated

the profound impact of environmental activism on social and economic development. By mobilizing women to plant millions of trees, Maathai addressed deforestation, environmental degradation, and gender inequality. Her holistic approach to development, which integrated environmental conservation with women's empowerment and social justice, earned her the Nobel Peace Prize and left a lasting legacy in sustainable development. Maathai's work underscores the interconnectedness of environmental sustainability, social equity, and economic resilience.

Emma Watson's advocacy for gender equality through the HeForShe campaign highlighted the importance of solidarity between genders in achieving social justice. By calling on men and boys to actively participate in the fight for gender equality, Watson expanded the feminist movement to be more inclusive and collaborative. Her use of digital platforms to engage with a global audience and her emphasis on intersectionality have contributed to a broader and more nuanced understanding of gender issues. Watson's work exemplifies how celebrity influence can be harnessed to drive social change and promote equality.

Hillary Clinton's declaration that "women's rights are human rights" during the 1995 Beijing Conference remains a cornerstone of the global gender equality movement. Throughout her career as First Lady, U.S. Senator, Secretary of State, and presidential candidate, Clinton consistently advocated for policies that promote gender equality and protect women's rights. Her leadership in initiatives such as the Violence Against Women Act and her emphasis on women's economic empowerment and political participation have significantly advanced the cause of women's rights globally. Clinton's legacy as a champion for women's rights continues to inspire and guide efforts toward gender equality.

Ellen Johnson Sirleaf's presidency in Liberia marked a period of stabilization and recovery for a nation ravaged by civil war. As Africa's first elected female head of state, Johnson Sirleaf implemented policies focused on rebuilding infrastructure, promoting economic development, and fostering national reconciliation. Her leadership during the Ebola crisis demonstrated her ability to navigate complex challenges with resilience and determination. Johnson Sirleaf's commitment to democratic governance, transparency, and women's empowerment has set a precedent for future leaders and highlighted the transformative potential of female leadership.

Shirin Ebadi's relentless advocacy for human rights in Iran has made her a symbol of resistance against authoritarianism. As one of the first female judges in Iran and later a Nobel Peace Prize laureate, Ebadi has dedicated her life to defending political dissidents, women, and children facing discrimination and persecution. Despite facing significant personal risk and being forced into exile, her work continues to shine a light on the systemic injustices in Iran and inspire global human rights movements. Ebadi's legacy underscores the importance of legal advocacy and grassroots activism in advancing human rights and justice.

The future of women's voices is inherently tied to the ongoing struggle for gender equality and social justice. Ensuring greater representation of women in all spheres of society, addressing systemic inequalities, leveraging technology, and fostering inclusive environments are critical steps toward amplifying women's voices. The intersectionality of gender with other social identities must be acknowledged and addressed to create a more inclusive feminist movement. Efforts to promote education, economic empowerment, and health and reproductive rights are fundamental to empowering women to participate fully in society.

The digital age offers unprecedented opportunities for women to connect, share their stories, and advocate for change. However, it also presents challenges such as online harassment and cyberbullying that must be addressed to ensure safe and inclusive digital spaces. Education remains a cornerstone of women's empowerment, providing the knowledge and skills needed to advocate for their rights and contribute to their communities. Economic empowerment, through addressing the gender pay gap and supporting women entrepreneurs, is essential for financial independence and social mobility.

Combating gender-based violence and discrimination is crucial for creating environments where women can advocate for their rights without fear of retribution. Health and reproductive rights are fundamental to women's autonomy and well-being, and ensuring access to comprehensive healthcare is vital for their participation in society. The arts and media play a significant role in shaping cultural narratives and promoting positive representations of women. Supporting women in creative industries and promoting diverse and authentic portrayals can help shift cultural perceptions and promote gender equality.

Policy advocacy and legal reforms are essential for advancing women's rights and creating a just and equitable society. Engaging with policymakers, building coalitions, and mobilizing communities are strategies for driving policy change. Legal reforms must be effectively implemented and enforced to ensure that women can access justice and hold perpetrators accountable. Global cooperation and solidarity are vital for addressing gender disparities and promoting women's empowerment. Collaborative efforts, such as the United Nations' Sustainable Development Goals, provide a framework for addressing global gender issues.

The journey toward gender equality is ongoing, and the voices of women will continue to be a driving force in shaping a more just and equitable world. The contributions of influential women like Michelle Obama, Greta Thunberg, Jacinda Ardern, Benazir Bhutto,

Wangari Maathai, Emma Watson, Hillary Clinton, Ellen Johnson Sirleaf, and Shirin Ebadi demonstrate the power of resilience, determination, and advocacy in effecting meaningful change. Their legacies serve as an inspiration and a guide for future generations of women leaders and activists, highlighting the importance of perseverance and the ongoing struggle for justice and equality. The future of women's voices is bright, and their continued advocacy will be instrumental in building a world where everyone, regardless of gender, can live with dignity, freedom, and equality.

Citation And References

This book represents the culmination of extensive research and meticulous analysis, incorporating a diverse range of sources, including numerous books, scholarly studies, and personal experiences. Additionally, I have scoured various websites to gather relevant information and data essential for the compilation of this work. I have taken every precaution to ensure the accuracy of the information presented and have diligently cited all sources to acknowledge their contributions.

Despite these efforts, the possibility of inadvertent errors remains. I deeply value the insights of my readers and appreciate any feedback that can help identify and rectify such inaccuracies. I encourage you to bring any discrepancies to my attention.

Your feedback is not only welcome but crucial, as it will aid in correcting current editions and enhancing the content of future ones. I am committed to maintaining the highest standards of accuracy and reliability in my work and thank you for your support and understanding.

Additionally, I firmly uphold the principle of freedom of speech and expression as guaranteed under Article 19(1)(a) of the Constitution of India, and I respect the diverse viewpoints and expressions of all readers.

ᗡᗡᗡ

Other Books Of The Author

1. Empowering Minds: A Journey into Women's Self-Discovery and Power
2. The Dynamics of Motivation: Catalyzing Thought into Action
3. Meditation and Mental Well Being: The Path to Inner Peace and Clarity
4. The Psychology of Child Education: Nurturing Future Generations
5. Ethical Enlightenment: A Modern Guide to Living with Integrity
6. Voices of Empowerment: Stories of Women Rising Against Odds
7. Social Psychology in Everyday Life: Understanding Human Connections
8. The Essence of Motivational Speaking: Inspiring Change in Others
9. Balancing Acts: Women, Work, and the Will to Lead
10. Guiding with Grace: Raising Children with Compassion and Awareness
11. The Power of Positive Aging: Embracing Life After Fifty
12. Building Resilient Communities: Social Work in Action
13. The Ethical Educator: Principles for Teaching and Learning
14. From Insight to Impact: Social Psychology for a Better World
15. The Ethics of Empathy: A Guide to Ethical Living
16. The Science of Empowering the Self: Navigating Life's Challenges with Psychological Wisdom
17. The Mindful Conscious Leader: Meditation Techniques for Modern Management
18. Pioneering Spirit: Women's Pathways to Leadership and Empowerment
19. Feeling to Healing: The Role of Emotional Intelligence in Child Development
20. Transformative Talks and Words of Inspiration: Insights into Motivational Oratory

21. Green Ethics: A Path to Sustainable Living
22. Spiritual Integrity: Navigating Life with Moral Compassion
23. Clean Living, Clean Society: The Ethics of Cleanliness
24. Patriotic Spirits: Building a Nation on Positive Attitudes
25. Innovative Integrity & Vibrant Visions: The Ethical and Entrepreneurial Spirit of Gujarat
26. Youthful Visions, Endless Possibilities: Inspiring Ethics and Motivation in Children
27. Living Your Legacy: How to Motivate Others by Living Your Values
28. Secret of Healing Conversations: Ethical Practices in Counselling and Therapy
29. Creative Kindness: Crafting a Life of Compassion and Creativity
30. The Power of Appreciation: How Gratitude Can Transform Your Relationships
31. Bhagavad-Gita: Messages
32. Science of Art: The New Frontier of Fashion Modernism
33. Vivekananda's Virtues: A Blueprint for Modern Living
34. Empower Her: Navigating the Path to Women's Entrepreneurship
35. The Boundless Classroom: Innovations in Global Education
36. The Language of Leadership: Communicating with Authenticity and Impact
37. The Warrior's Mantra: Deciphering the Hanuman Chalisa
38. Echoes of Empathy: Transformative Stories of Social Service
39. Artful Living: Cultivating Creativity in Your Daily Routine
40. Finding Your Why: Discovering Your Passions and Charting Your Course
41. The Role of Social Media in Shaping Self-Esteem and Interpersonal Relationships among Adolescents
42. Karma's Tapestry: Weaving a Life of Selfless Service
43. Altruistic Alchemy: Transforming Lives Through Giving
44. The Blueprint of Pro-Activeness and Productivity: Crafting Habits for Success
45. The Simplicity with Grounded Wisdom: Embracing Authenticity

in a Complex World

46. Secret of Solopreneur's Odyssey: Navigating the Path to Self-Employment
47. Exploring Tapestry of Peace: Global Perspectives on Harmony
48. The Art and Actions of Connection: Mastering Communication for Impact
49. She Governs and at the Helm: Strategies for Political Empowerment
50. Rising Above and Rising with Grace: A Woman's Roadmap to Career Mastery
51. The Effect of Networking & Connectedness: Building Strategic Alliances for Women
52. Beyond his Barriers: Women Thriving in Male-Dominated Fields
53. Secret of Inner Compass: Navigating Life with Intuition
54. Creative & Pro-Active Muses: A Celebration of Women in the Arts
55. Unburdened: The Art of Releasing the Past
56. Amplified Voices: Speeches of Women that Astonished the World
57. Secret of Manifesting Dreams: A Woman's Guide to Intentional Living
58. Ethics and Value Based Education: Reimagining Japan's School System
59. The Moral Compass Curriculum: A Holistic Approach
60. Tech with Heart: Integrating Ethics into Digital Learning
61. Honoring Virtue: Recognizing Ethical Excellence in Education
62. Raising Good Humans: A Guide to Character Development
63. The Spark Within: Nurturing Creativity in Children
64. The Teenager Whisperer: Navigating Adolescence with Grace
65. Igniting a Passion for Learning: Inspiring Lifelong Curiosity
66. The Habit Lab: Cultivating Positive Behaviors in Children
67. Seeds of Empathy: Fostering Compassion in Young Hearts
68. The Reading Revolution: Inspiring a Love of Books in Children
69. The Learning Brain: Unlocking the Secrets of Student Success
70. Teaching for All: Differentiated Instruction Strategies
71. The Time Alchemist: Mastering Time Management for Peak Performance

72. The Resilience Factor: Transforming Setbacks into Stepping Stones
73. The Healing Touch of Nature: An Introduction to Naturopathy
74. Echoes of the Past: Healing Through Past Life Regression
75. The Spiritual Healer's Handbook: Exploring Energy Medicine
76. Crystal Clarity: Unveiling the Power of Gemstones
77. The Dream Weaver's Guide: Decoding the Language of Dreams
78. Emotional Alchemy: Transforming Pain into Power
79. Sonic Serenity: Harnessing Sound for Stress Relief
80. The Entrepreneur's Playbook: Launching Your Business with Confidence
81. Productivity Unleashed: Time Management Strategies for Entrepreneurs
82. The Problem Solver's Toolkit: Creative Solutions for Business Challenges
83. The Future is Now: Emerging Trends in Business
84. The Curious Explorer: A Child's Guide to Scientific Discovery
85. Digital Pioneers: Empowering Kids in the Tech World
86. The Young Philosopher's Guide: Exploring Life's Big Questions
87. Finding Your Voice: Communication Skills for Confident Kids
88. Nature's Playground: A Child's Guide to Outdoor Adventure
89. Growing a Greener Tomorrow: A Guide to Tree Planting & Conservation
90. Driving with Purpose: Ethical Choices on the Road
91. The Healing Touch: Cultivating Compassion in Healthcare
92. Navigating the Digital Landscape: Ethics in the Age of Social Media
93. The Ethical Closet: A Guide to Sustainable Fashion
94. The Mindful Voyager: Sustainable Travel Practices
95. The Feminine Divine: Honoring the Goddesses of India
96. Sacred Sounds: Chanting Your Way to Inner Peace
97. The Yoga Path: Uniting with the Divine Within
98. Rites of Passage: Creating Meaningful Ceremonies
99. The Chakra System: A Map of Inner Transformation
100. Spiritual Sangha: Finding Community through Satsang and

Bhajan

101. Pilgrimage of the Soul: Spiritual Journeys in India

ÞÞÞ

Contact

Dr. Minakshi Bansal
Social Activist
Ahmedabad, Gujarat, Bharat
minakshiindiag20@yahoo.com

❦❦❦

|| LOKAHA SAMASTHAHA SUKHINO BHAVANTU ||